Callagrass Cuisine
2014

Compiled and Cooked by Joan Callaway

ii

CONTENTS

December 15, 2014

Dear Friends and Family,

We hope you'll enjoy these recipes as much as we do. At one time or another, we've shared every recipe included here with dear friends and family (all dear friends, too, of course) and the fellowship has been as enjoyable as the dining. We always think that good food enhances the experience.

The recipes come from a variety of sources, but most have been adapted to reflect our tastes, lifestyle, and lighter dietary desires. My penchant for elegant gourmet cuisine and watching PBS cooking shows on Saturdays, as well as my spirit of adventure at least when it comes to cooking, will undoubtedly come through in this cookbook.

You'll also see some attempt to balance great meals with very busy schedules. Most of the time, I started dinner when Ed phoned me with the "Home Again, Home Again" message, letting me know he is walking out the door at the airport. This means that most of the meals can be prepared in half an hour or less.

In many of the recipes, I've replaced specific measurements with "salt to taste" because I've reduced the amount of salt we use.

Not that these recipes are necessarily to be considered the foundation of a healthy diet, although most have lots of fresh vegetables, are low in fats, sugar and all that good stuff we're supposed to give up. But some of the special dishes like the Heartline Café Crème Brulée, could really get you into trouble if you ate them regularly. But then, that's why they are so special!

The point is, these are foods that we've enjoyed together and we thought that sharing them with you was the best way to thank you for your love, friendship, and support over the years. Enjoy!

iii

1

EARLY RISERS

Gigi's Nutty Granola

-
-
-
-
-

- 3-4 or 5 cups oatmeal
- to 1 ½ cups mixed nuts (I use walnuts, pecans, almonds and cashews, depending on what I have in the freezer), chopped
- ½ cup maple syrup
- ½ cup sunflower seeds
- ½ cup wheat germ (optional)

Mix all together and spread on cookie sheet with sides. Toast in 325=350 degree oven for 15 minutes. Stir. And bake for another 10-15 minutes to desired toastiness.

Cool and add banana chips. Dried fruit added and then stored tends to get more dried and chewy. Probably better to add gradually as you eat it. I like to add dried cranberries, dried cherries, blueberries, etc. Fresh fruit and Greek yogurt are nice additions, so I sometimes leave off the dried fruit.

I especially like Greek yogurt with raspberries and a little granola on the top for a bit of a crunch.

Banana Walnut Pancakes or Waffles

Prepare your favorite pancake mix or recipe. Ours is Krusteaz! Add 1 sliced banana, ½ cup finely chopped walnuts, and ¼ tsp. Cinnamon. Bake on griddle or waffle iron as usual. Serve with heated maple syrup.

Rum Raisin French Toast

¾ cup rum raisin ice cream, melted
3 eggs, beaten just until blended
½ cup ground walnuts
1 Tbsp. Amber rum ¼
tsp. Cinnamon
8 slices raisin bread

4 Tbsp. Butter
Maple syrup
Additional rum raisin ice cream (not melted)

Combine melted ice cream with eggs, walnuts, rum and cinnamon in a large shallow pan or bowl. Dip raisin bread into mixture and let soak one minute per side.
Melt 2 Tbsp. Butter in heavy skillet over medium heat or in electric fry pan. Place four bread slices in pan and cook until brown, about 2 minutes per side. Repeat with remaining bread. Serve immediately with maple syrup and topped with a small scoop of ice cream. Serves 4

Ham Biscuits with Honey Clove Butter

3 cups Bisquick
½ stick margarine or butter
Milk (approximately ¾ cup)
¼ # sliced ham, chopped fine

Mix together – just until it holds together. Gather the dough into a ball and knead gently a few times on a lightly floured surface. Roll or pat out ½ inch thick. Cut out as many rounds as possible with a 3" cookie cutter (or small glass) dipped in flour. Transfer onto ungreased baking sheet. Gather the scraps, re-roll the dough, and cut out until dough is used up. Brush the tops with milk and bake in a preheated 425-degree oven until lightly browned…15 minutes.

Honey-Clove Butter:

Make honey clove butter while biscuits are baking: In a small bowl cream together:

½ stick butter
1/8 tsp. Ground cloves
1 tsp. honey
Pinch of salt

Serve with Teedy's warm biscuits. (See Teedy's Biscuits in Breads chapter) Note: Since we have moved to University Retirement Center in Davis, we have not made Eggs Benedict. It is served every Wednesday morning in the Deli and on Sundays at Brunch. But if we were to have it at home, this would be the recipe we'd use. It's the fresh lemon juice that makes this Hollandaise Sauce!

Hollandaise Sauce for Eggs Benedict

(Easy and fool-proof!)

4 tsp. Unsalted butter
½ c. water
1 egg yolk
1 T. fresh lemon juice
½ tsp. Dijon mustard
½ T. flour
½ tsp. Salt
Finely grated zest of one lemon

Melt the butter in a small saucepan over medium heat. Whisk the water, egg yolk, lemon juice, mustard and salt in small bowl; gradually add the flour. Whisk this mixture into the butter, stirring constantly. Bring to a boil and stir about 45 seconds. Remove from the heat and stir in the lemon zest. Makes ½ cup, providing 2 Tbsp. serving over each poached egg, Canadian bacon, and English muffin half. WW: 1 point for sauce.

To poach an egg, bring enough water to cover the egg, along with a couple of teaspoons of vinegar to a simmer. Break each egg into a small bowl or cup and then drop gently into the simmering water. The vinegar helps the egg whites to stay together rather than spreading out all over the pan. Continue to simmer until whites of eggs are cooked, but yolks are still "dippy," as my grandkids say – runny enough to dip toast into.

Bacon – This is the way they cook it at the URC Deli…nice flat crispy pieces!

1. Turn on your oven to 400 degrees. Line a rimmed baking sheet with foil. Use heavy duty if you have it. Lay out bacon slices in a single layer. They can be close together, just avoid overlap. You can also place a metal cooling rack in your pan and lay the bacon on top of that. Personally I think it tastes way better when it cooks up in its own drippings!

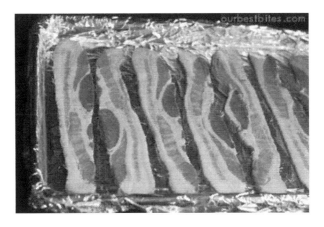

2. You don't need to wait for your oven to preheat. Place pan in the oven for about 12-15 minutes. Watch bacon after that and cook until desired level of crispiness. I like mine on the crispy side so I cook it for about 15-17 minutes. Cooking time depends on the thickness of the slice as well.

Fireman's Brunch Casserole

The night before: Butter heavily the bottom and sides of a 9 x 15 inch baking dish…or larger. Cut crusts off approximately 20 slices of white bread and butter one side of ten of the slices. Place the ten unbuttered slices in bottom of dish. Cover with toasted sesame seeds, finely chopped green onions, cooked Jimmy Dean pre-seasoned breakfast sausage, and shredded mild or medium Cheddar cheese. Repeat the layering process using the buttered slices for the top layer.

Mix slightly 16 large eggs (fewer if extra-large) and about a cup of milk. Pour over ingredients in baking dish. It should come to top of dish. Cover with Saran wrap and refrigerate overnight.

In the morning: Preheat oven to 325 degrees and place casserole in pan of water in the oven for one hour or until lightly browned. (The water in the pan keeps the mixture moist. It is custard-like, but firmer.)

Variations: Add crab or shrimp (Great for brunch!)
Chopped chilies, ham and green pepper.
      Gruyere cheese or jack and mozzarella combined
      Mushrooms
Imagination!

Christmas morning mimosas

Poppyseed Bread

4 eggs   1 ½ c. oil
1 ½ tsp. Soda   3c.flour
½ tsp. Salt
2 cups sugar   1 large can evaporated milk
½ c. chopped walnuts
2-3 T. Poppy seeds

Mix well. Prepare a 9x4" baking pan. Bake at 350 degrees 45 minutes to one hour. I often put in mini loaf pans for gift giving or as individual loaves for brunch, and these take less baking time. (Test with toothpick to determine doneness!)

Russian Tea

2 cups Tang
1 cup instant tea 1 package of
Wiley's Lemonade mix
1 tsp. cinnamon
1/2 tsp. cloves
1 1/4 cup sugar

Joni's Nut Rolls   For that special brunch!

Mix together:

1 c. lukewarm water
¼ c. sugar
1 tsp. Salt

Crumble into the mixture 1 cake yeast or 1 package dry yeast. Stir until yeast is dissolved. Beat in:

1 egg
¼ c. soft shortening

Mix in with spoon by hand 3 ½ to 3 ¾ cups sifted flour. Add in two parts until dough is easy to handle. Turn out onto lightly floured board. Cover with a damp cloth and let rest 10 minutes. Knead until smooth and elastic. Round up and place in greased bowl. Cover with a damp cloth and let rise until double in bulk at approximately 85 degrees. Push down and let rise again until double in bulk.

Pour out onto floured cloth or board and let rest 15 minutes. Roll out into 14x20" rectangle. Spread with ¼ cup softened butter. Sprinkle with ½ cup finely chopped nuts. Fold over in thirds and then make ½" slices, twisting them into butter horn shape (coils) or knots. Let rise for 30 minutes. Bake 10-12 minutes at 425 degrees. Frost with ¾ c. powdered sugar, 1 T. milk or orange juice with orange zest. Glaze while still hot.

German Oven Pancake

½ c. sifted flour
3 slightly beaten eggs
½ c. milk   2 Tbsp. Melted butter
¼ tsp. salt   powdered sugar
Lemon wedges

Gradually add flour to eggs, beat. Stir in milk, melted butter and salt. Thoroughly grease a 9 x 10" cast iron skillet (preferably). Pour batter into cold skillet and bake in very hot oven – 450 degrees – about 20 minutes. Cut into wedges. Sprinkle with powdered sugar and garnish with lemon wedges.

Potato Pancakes (Latkes)

1 medium potato for each person, grated
1 small onion, grated
1 egg for every three potatoes
1 T. flour for every three potatoes
Salt, pepper, paprika

Stir liquid ingredients together with potatoes that have been well drained after grating. Using a slotted spoon, drain off the excess liquid from a large spoonful. Drop into ½ inch hot oil and flatten. Cook until golden brown. Drain on paper towel to remove oil. (If these are cooked fairly rapidly, they do not absorb much fat.)

Serve with sour cream and applesauce for brunch or light supper.

Ashland Raspberry Cobbler

I usually prepare this for dessert, but somehow kids and adults alike always hope there are leftovers for breakfast, so why not just MAKE it for brunch/breakfast entrée, as well as dessert.

Serving Size: 8

- 1 stick Butter
- 1-1/4 cup Sugar
- 1 cup Self-Rising Flour
- 1 cup Milk
- 2 cups Blackberries (frozen Or Fresh)

Melt butter in a microwavable dish. Pour 1 cup of sugar and self-rising flour into a mixing bowl, whisking in milk. Mix well. Then, pour in melted butter and whisk it all well together. Butter a baking dish.

Now rinse and pat dry the blackberries. Pour the batter into the buttered baking dish. Sprinkle blackberries over the top of the batter; distributing evenly. Sprinkle ¼ cup sugar over the top.

Bake in the oven at 350 degrees for 1 hour, or until golden and bubbly. If you desire, sprinkle an additional teaspoon of sugar over the cobbler 10 minutes before it's done.

Joan's Blueberry Scones

1 ½ cups reduced-fat Bisquick®
1   egg
1/3 – 1/2 cup yogurt or buttermilk to make a batter for a loose spoon biscuit
– thicker than for cake, but between thicker than cake consistency, but too
sticky for rolling out. Clear?.
2   tablespoons sugar
3/4 cup blueberries
1/2 lemon - zest only

Glaze:
    Powdered sugar
    Lemon juice
    Lemon zest

1.Preheat oven to 400 degrees.
2.Spoon batter onto prepared cookie sheet and bake for 20 minutes. Note:
This batter is too gooey to roll out. Just mound them up.
3.Drizzle lemon glaze over the top while they are still warm.
"Double recipe for four people"

One of my favorite kitchen tools

Microplane for grating lemon or cheese

Banana Bread

3 ripe bananas
2 cups all-purpose flour
1 tsp. salt
1 tsp. baking powder
1 tsp. baking soda
½ cup soft butter
1 cup sugar
2 large eggs
¼ tsp. vanilla
1 Tbsp. milk
1 cup chopped walnuts
1/3 cup dark chocolate chips

Add eggs, sugar and softened butter to smashed bananas. Mix in dry ingredients.

Bake in 9 x 4" loaf pan at 325 degrees F. for about 1 hour and 10 minutes. Cool before slicing.

2
LIFE OF THE PARTY
HORS D'OEUVRES & APPETIZERS

Crab Canapés

8 oz. package butter flake rolls (or some that can be divided into 36 pieces) 1 8oz. can water chestnuts, drained and sliced

Combine the following:

1 7 ½ oz. can or fresh crabmeat
1 Tbsp. chopped green onions
4 oz. shredded Swiss cheese
½ c. mayonnaise
¼ tsp. curry powder
1 tsp. lemon juice

Separate each butter flake roll into three pieces (36 in all), placing them on greased baking sheet. Spoon on crabmeat mixture. Top with slice of water chestnut. Bake at 400 degrees – 12 minutes. Serve hot. May be reheated.

(Note: Make plenty because I've seen guests follow a tray of these around the living room like starving vultures.)

Cream Cheese and Chilies Dip

- 1 chopped tomato
- 1 chopped onion
- 1 minced clove garlic
- 1 or 2 small cans diced jalapenos
- 1 large package cream cheese

Sauté first three ingredients. Add chilies and cream cheese. Stir until cream cheese melts. Keep warm in chafing dish and serve with tortilla chips.

Note: Mark made this often when he was in high school

Curried Chicken Wings

Remove tips from 24 chicken wings. Cut other part of wing in two, creating two mini-drumsticks. Use tips for stock or discard. Marinate mini-drumsticks in the following:

- 6-8 peeled yellow onions, diced
- 2 cloves garlic, minced
- 1 tsp. each: salt, pepper
- 1 Tbsp. Curry powder
- ½ c. sour cream

Melt ¼ c. butter in shallow baking pan. Transfer wings with whatever marinade clings to them to pan. Bake and hour or so until nicely browned in 375-degree oven, turning occasionally. Serve at once.

Marinated Chicken Wings...or anything

- 1 cup soy sauce
- ½ c. red wine
- Shot of brandy (optional)
- 3 green onions, tops and all, chopped
- 1 clove garlic, minced
- ½ c. water
- 1/3 cup sugar

Marinate for 3 to 4 hours. Bake 40 – 45 minutes at 400 degrees until glossy looking.

Broiled Clam Canapés

1 can minced clams, drained
¼ pint whipping cream, whipped
1 T. finely chopped onion
1 – 8 oz. package cream cheese
1 tsp. lemon juice
½ clove garlic, pressed
Tobasco – dash
Salt, pepper

Using a cookie cutter make bread rounds from white sliced bread. Toast lightly under broiler or in Teflon fry pan. Spread with clam mixture. Broil until lightly browned and bubbly. Serve at once.

Delicious Little Thingies – Jalapeno Poppers

Fresh Jalapeno peppers – 2-3" long
Cream cheese
Bacon

Slice peppers in half lengthwise.
Remove seeds and white membranes with spoon.
Cut bacon into thirds.
Smear softened cream cheese inside each pepper half.
Wrap bacon around snugly, but not too tightly.
Stick toothpick through middle of each one.
Place on rack on cookie sheet.
Bake in preheated 375 degree oven for 20-25 minutes
until bacon is crispy.

Open Sesame Appetizer Meatballs (Mike Henry's Choice)

- 2 T. butter
- 2 T. flour
- 1/4 tsp. salt
- Dash cayenne
- 1/2 c. beef broth
- 1 tsp. soy sauce
- 1 tsp. Worcestershire Sauce
- 2 T. toasted sesame seeds
- 1 c. sour cream
- 1 recipe of Tasty Meat Balls (below)

Melt butter on medium heat. Blend in next three ingredients. Stir until
bubbly. Add broth all at once and cook, stirring until sauce thickens. Stir in
next three ingredients. Gradually add hot sauce to sour cream, stirring
constantly. Return sauce to pan. Fold in meatballs and heat to serving
temperature. Serve from chafing dish with toothpicks. Makes about 60.

Basic Tasty Appetizer Meatball

- 2/3 c. minced onion
- 1 # lean ground beef (or turkey)
- ½ cup soft bread crumbs (1 slice)
- 1 egg
- ¼ cup milk
- ½ tsp. salt
- 1/8 tsp. pepper
- 1 Tbsp. Worcestershire sauce

Mix above ingredients and shape into small one-inch meatballs. Fry in hot cooking oil ¾" deep, until lightly browned. The meatballs do not need to be turned. Remove from pan. Simmer in 1-cup beef broth, bouillon or consommé about ten minutes. (Note: these can be frozen loose on a cookie sheet and wrapped when solid for later use. Thaw in microwave or 300 degree oven before adding to your choice of sauce.)

Pita Wedges

6 pieces of Pita bread
½ cup olive oil
3 T. Kosher salt

Cut pita into 6 wedges. Spread in single layer on cookie sheet (foil for easy clean-up) Bruch both sides generously with olive oil. Sprinkle lightly with Kosher salt. Bake for 15-18 minutes in 375 degree oven or until desired color.

Spinach Artichoke Dip (Pioneer Woman)
3 Tablespoons Butter
4 Tablespoons Garlic, Minced
1 bag Spinach
Salt And Pepper, to taste
2 cans Artichoke Hearts, Rinsed And Drained
3 Tablespoons Butter (additional)
3 Tablespoons Flour
1-1/2 cup Whole Milk (more If Needed)
1 package (8 Ounce) Softened Cream Cheese
1/2 cup Crumbled Feta
1/2 cup Grated Parmesan
3/4 cups Grated Pepper Jack Cheese
1/4 teaspoon Cayenne
Extra Grated Pepper Jack
Pita Wedges, Tortilla Chips, Crackers

Melt 3 tablespoons butter in a skillet over medium heat. Add the minced garlic and cook for a couple of minutes. Add spinach, stir and cook for a couple of minutes until spinach wilts. Remove the spinach from the skillet. Excess liquid back into pan. Add artichokes and cook over medium high heat for several minutes, until liquid is cooked off and artichokes start to get a little color. Remove the artichokes.

In the same skillet, melt 3 additional tablespoons of butter and whisk in 3 tablespoons of flour until it makes a paste. Cook over medium-low heat for a minute or two, then pour in milk. Stir and cook until slightly thickened; splash in more milk if needed.

Add cream cheese, feta, Parmesan, pepper jack, and cayenne and stir until cheese are melted and sauce is smooth. Chop artichokes and spinach and add to the sauce. Stir to combine.

Pour into buttered baking dish. Top with extra grated pepper jack and bake at 375 for 15 minutes, or until cheese is melted and bubbly.

Serve with pita wedges, chips, or crackers!

Turkey Meatballs - Appetizer or Entrée

- 1 pound ground turkey
- 1/2 cup oatmeal
- 1/4 cup chopped onion
- 1/4 cup grated Parmesan cheese
- 2 tablespoons chopped parsley
- 2 teaspoons minced garlic
- 2 large egg white -- beaten and frothy
- 1/2 teaspoon salt
- 1/2 teaspoon oregano
- 1/2 teaspoon basil
- 1/4 teaspoon pepper
- 1 1/2 cups chicken stock

In a large bowl combine turkey, oatmeal, onion, Parmesan cheese, garlic, beaten egg whites, salt, oregano, basil and pepper. Mix lightly, but thoroughly.

With moistened hands, lightly shape mixture into 1-inch balls. You should end up with about 36 balls. Bring the chicken stock to a simmer and drop meatballs in, leaving space between. Simmer until they are cooked on outside, turning occasionally as needed. Remove from stock and put in baking dish. Bake in 350-degree oven until lightly browned.
Yield: 4 servings of 9 meatballs each = WW 5 Points

- - - - - - - - - - - - - - - - - -

Three of the leftover meatballs inside a pita bread with tomato, onion and a bit of fat free cottage cheese, heated slightly in microwave, makes a delightful filling

Oysters Dunbar

I was never able to talk Corinne Dunbar Restaurant in New Orleans into giving me the recipe, but I think mine comes pretty close.

4 T. butter	4 green onions, diced
3 T, flour	½ bottle clam juice
1 jar oysters	1 package frozen artichoke hearts
1/8 tsp. salt	1/8 tsp. pepper
Dash Tabasco	

Sauté green onions in butter. Add flour to make a roux. Add oyster water, and if needed additional clam juice or water. Cook a little while. Add very small oysters (or ones that have been cut into bite-sized pieces, boiled artichoke hearts that have been cut into same size as oysters, along with some of the scrapings from the leaves if you have started from scratch. Season to taste with salt, pepper and a bit of Tabasco. Cook all about ten minutes.

Then drop this insipid looking goo into a small ramekin (I use a small shell from Cost Plus), cover with buttered bread crumbs/Parmesan cheese mixture…and place in hot oven for browning. (You can make these ahead and reheat when you plan to serve. This is an excellent first course with a dry white wine. I guarantee your guests will scrape their plates – even if they had thought they didn't like oysters.

Baked Brie

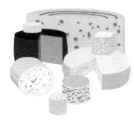

1 (3oz) round of Brie Cheese

1 small package of refrigerated crescent rolls

1 egg, beaten

- Crescent rolls from refrigerated case in supermarket
- Brie
- Sliced apples and pears
- Sourdough bread or crackers

Unroll crescent rolls and pinch together perforations. Wrap around Brie and pinch closed. Decorate with extra dough. Place on oiled baking sheet. Brush top with beaten egg. Bake at 375 degrees for 10 to 15 minutes or until golden brown.

Remove to serving dish or cutting board. Let cool about 5 minutes before cutting. Slice into sections and serve with sliced apples and pears, etc.

Chocolate Dipped Strawberries

1 package semi-sweet chocolate chips
Large ripe, but firm, strawberries

Quick Microwave Recipe: In a microwavable bowl, melt chocolate chips at Low power for a few minutes. If using full power, zap for two minutes, checking consistency. Continue to melt in two-minute intervals until chips can be stirred smooth.

Be sure that your strawberries are completely dry after washing. Dip half to 2/3 strawberry in chocolate and place in pastry cup or on waxed paper.

Stuffed Artichokes

4 medium artichokes
½ lemon
¾ c. plain dried bread crumbs
2 Tbsp. Chopped Parsley
2 Tbsp. Chopped basil
2 Tbsp. Chopped tarragon
1 tsp. Lemon zest
2 Tbsp. Lemon juice
½ tsp. Chopped rosemary
½ tsp. Salt
¼ freshly ground pepper
Finely minced garlic, to taste (optional)
Enough olive oil to just moisten lightly

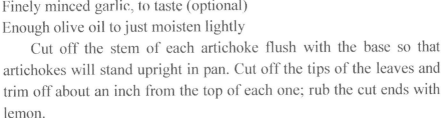

Cut off the stem of each artichoke flush with the base so that artichokes will stand upright in pan. Cut off the tips of the leaves and trim off about an inch from the top of each one; rub the cut ends with lemon.

Fill a large non-reactive pan with 8 cups of water, then add artichokes and lemon; bring to a boil. Reduce heat and simmer for 15 to 20 minutes. [Note: Like apples and pears, artichokes will turn brown if they're not dropped in acidulated water or rubbed with lemon. Adding what's left of the lemon to the cooking water helps to retain their color. I usually sprinkle tops with a bit of salt, too.

Meanwhile, preheat oven to 350 degrees and prepare bread crumb mixture. Toss to combine remaining ingredients.

When artichokes appear tender – pull a leaf. If it comes off easily, they are done. Remove center leaves and choke in center of artichoke before stuffing with the breadcrumb mixture. Stuff in and around leaves, too. Place on baking sheet. Bake until the bread crumbs are nicely browned…15 minutes or so.

Salami and Cheese Rolls: Stromboli

1 pound frozen supermarket pizza dough -- thawed
1/4 cup finely grated Parmigiano-Reggiano
Freshly ground black pepper
3 ounces thinly sliced salami (about 12 slices)
4 ounces thinly sliced provolone (about 12 slices)
 2/3 cup jarred roasted bell peppers -- rinsed and chopped 1
large egg -- lightly beaten

Preheat oven to 400 degrees F.

Quarter dough. Roll out 1 piece into a 10-inch round on a lightly floured surface and sprinkle evenly with 1 tablespoon Parmesan and black pepper, to taste. Arrange 1/4 each of salami, provolone, and roasted peppers in an even layer over dough. Roll up dough round, then tuck ends under and pinch edges to seal.

Make 3 more rolls in same manner and arrange 2 inches apart on a lightly greased baking sheet. Brush lightly with egg and cut 3 (1/2-inch) steam vents in each roll. Bake in middle of oven until golden, 30 to 35 minutes.

Sara's Note: For all you college students, this is great recipe for your dormroom toaster oven. Bake them up and you'll be the envy of all your dormmates.

3
JOAN'S FAVORITE SOUPS

Grandpa Jack's Dieter's Meal in One Vegetable Soup

      1 Tbsp. Olive oil
- 2 cloves garlic, minced
- 1 stalk celery, sliced
- 1 bell pepper, seeded and cut into pieces
- unscraped carrots, sliced
- 3 unpeeled red potatoes, sliced
- 1 cup yellow squash, cubed
- 1 zucchini, cut into rounds
- 2 leaves of spinach or romaine
- 2-c. fresh tomatoes or #1 can diced tomatoes
- 2 quarts chicken stock 1 T. celery leaves
- 1 tsp. oregano
- 1 tsp. basil
- ¼ - ½ tsp. cayenne or Tabasco, to taste
- Pasta, optional
- 2 T. parsley

Set your timer for one hour and begin. Over the lowest heat in a 6-qt. pot, place oil and vegetables in order given. As you add the veggies, you can turn up the heat. Stir. By the time you get to the tomatoes, the pot will be half full. Cook and stir for a few minutes. Now add the liquids and seasonings. Keep the heat on high until you have a full rolling boil. Lower heat and simmer gently, uncovered for the remainder of the hour. About ten minutes before the hour is up, you can add the pasta if you like. Cover and let stand until ready to eat. Serve with a dusting of Parmesan cheese. Great the second day…and it freezes well. A little French bread and you have a meal in itself. (If you add pasta, you may need a bit more liquid …and it will not freeze as well.)

My Favorite Lentil Soup

2 large onions, diced
3 carrots, small dice or grated
3/4 tsp. marjoram, crumbled
3/4 tsp. thyme leaves, crumbled
28 oz. can chopped tomatoes with juice
7 cups chicken or vegie stock
1 ½ cups. Dried lentils
½ tsp. salt
Parsley

Sauté **2 large onions (2 cups)** and **3 diced carrots** in a tiny bit of olive oil (or water). Add **¾ tsp. Crumbled marjoram** and **¾ tsp. Crumbled thyme leaves**. Stir and sauté for about 5 minutes. Add one (28 oz.,) can chopped tomatoes with juice, 7 cups of broth, and 1 ½ c. dried lentils that have been rinsed and picked over or Bob's Red Mill Vegi Soup Mix (which I get through www.amazon.com. Bring the soup to a boil, reduce heat. Cover and simmer for about one hour or until lentils are tender. Add ½ tsp. Salt and pepper to taste, 6 oz. White wine (optional) and 1/3 c. chopped fresh parsley and simmer for another few minutes. Serve with grated Cheddar, Parmesan or Asiago cheese sprinkled on each portion.

Puerto Rican Black Bean Soup

4-6 cups chicken stock (bouillon cubes) ¼ c. vinegar
2 cups rinsed black beans   1 tsp. orange or lemon peel
½ c. chopped celery   ½ tsp. cinnamon
2 large carrots, diced   pinch cayenne – to taste
1 med. Yellow onion, diced   2 tsp. garlic, finely chopped

   Start with 4 cups of stock…and add more as needed, depending on whether you want soupy soup or a side dish with brown rice. Liquid made with bouillon cubes is okay for this soup. Put all ingredients together in a pot and cook slowly for three hours.
   Serve with cooked brown rice in bottom of bowl with the following garnishes to be added to taste: non-fat sour cream or yogurt, chopped green onions, chopped red onions, chopped tomatoes, chopped parsley, salsa. Serve with French bread, warm tortillas, or tostado shells.

Marci, Val and Laurie in Ashland

Sweet Potato and Corn Chowder with Roasted Peppers

(From Heartline Café in Sedona)

Six to 8 servings

2 cups sweet corn kernels
1 sweet potato, peeled and diced
1 Idaho white baking potato
1 Tbsp. Olive oil
1 tsp. chili powder
½ tsp. coriander
¾ tsp. ground cumin
½ tsp. black pepper
¾ tsp. kosher salt
1 medium white onion, peeled and diced
1   large carrot, peeled and diced
2   stalks celery, diced
3   ½ cup butter

2 tsp. minced garlic
   ½ c. roasted red peppers
4 cups chicken stock
4 cups heavy cream

1/3 cup butter, optional
½ c. flour (optional)

Preheat oven to 400 degrees. Toss corn kernels, peeled and diced sweet potato and white potato in olive oil with the chili powder, coriander, cumin, salt and pepper. Spread on cookie sheet and roast in oven, turning occasionally, until golden brown, about 25 minutes. Remove from oven and set aside.

Meanwhile, in large stockpot, sauté onion, carrot and celery in butter, stirring occasionally, until onions become translucent. Add the garlic roasted peppers and roasted veggies. Sauté for 5 minutes more. Add the chicken stock and half of the cream and simmer for 20 minutes. Add the remaining cream and simmer until volume has reduced by one-fourth. Season with salt and pepper to taste.For a thicker soup, cook one-third cup butter with onethird cup flour for about five minutes, and then whisk this mixture into the simmering soup and cook for five minutes. Serve with fresh cilantro as a garnish (or parsley). This can be stored in refrigerator for up to one week…but it is so delicious, it's doubtful there'll be any left. Well worth the effort and the calories once in a while. A favorite at our house!

Roasted Peppers (This makes enough for two batches of soup.)

1 Anaheim chili
½ red bell pepper
½ yellow bell pepper
1 Chipotle from a jar or can of chipotles in adobo, chopped
1 Tbsp. Olive oil
½ tsp. kosher salt

Place Anaheim and bell pepper on baking sheet and sprinkle with olive oil and salt. Bake at 400 degrees until peppers are blackened and skins look blistered and burned – about 20 minutes. Remove from oven and place in a covered bowl or paper bag. This allows pepper to steam, making their skins much easier to remove. When cool, about 20 minutes, peel, slice thinly and add chipotle. Chop finely.

Caprial's Butternut Squash Soup

1 large butternut squash (or two smaller), peeled, diced and roasted 1
  Tablespoon olive oil

2 large onions
 6 cloves garlic
 ½ cup dry sherry
 1 Tablespoon Worcestershire sauce
 1 Teaspoon cayenne sauce   (or to taste)
2 teaspoons fresh thyme
 2 teaspoons fresh oregano
Salt
Pepper
 8 cups non-fat chicken stock (or veggie)
 1/2 pound turkey Italian sausage -- browned and drained, cut into bite-sized
pieces (optional)

Peel and dice squash and coat with 1 Tablespoons olive oil. (I don't use this
much oil.)   Bake in 350-degree oven for 30 minutes until tender; sauté
onions in butter. Add garlic, roasted squash and sherry or Marsala wine, and
cook over high heat until reduced by one half. Add stock and bring to boil,
reduce heat to low and simmer 10 - 15 minutes. Meanwhile brown sausage,
if added (chorizo or hot Italian sausage.) Drain well.

Puree the solids and return to the stockpot with the liquid. Stir in sausage.
Add Worcestershire sauce, cayenne sauce, thyme and oregano, season to
taste with salt and pepper.

Serve with spicy cinnamon croutons (see below) – optional.

Spicy Cinnamon Croutons Makes
4 cups

¼ cup butter

1 cup firmly packed brown sugar

1 teaspoon chili powder

1 teaspoon ground cinnamon

1 baguette or loaf of sourdough bread cut into 1/2-inch cubes

Preheat the oven to 350 degrees. Melt butter in a sauté pan over medium heat. Stir in the brown sugar, chili powder and cinnamon and cook 2 to 3 minutes, or until bubbly. Transfer to a large bowl. Add the bread and toss to evenly coat. Spread the croutons on a sheet pan and bake until crispy and caramelized, 25 to 30 minutes. (Check after 15 minutes!) Remove the croutons from the oven and cool on a wire rack. (Don't worry if they stick together - they will break apart when cooled.)

Seafood Chowder

6 large potatoes, diced

1 medium onion, diced

2 cups water +/-

   Simmer until potatoes are nearly done. Remove 1 – 2 cups cooked potatoes with a bit of liquid to blender and puree. Return to potato mixture. Add **1/2 # scallops, 1/2 # fresh shrimp** peeled, deveined and chopped in three pieces, to potatoes and simmer gently until done.

Add **2 cans chopped clams with juice**. Add extra bottled clam juice for richer flavor. Add **crab** or any other **seafood** you choose. (Optional) Add **2 cans evaporated milk**. Thicken a bit with flour/water mixture (or flour/butter balls for thicker soup.

Cauliflower Cheese Chowder

4 cups diced cauliflower, including tender parts of the core.
1 cup chopped onion
½ cup chopped celery
1 cup chopped tomato, fresh or canned
2 ½ cups water

1 ½ tsp. Salt
2 Tbsp. Parsley
¼ c. whole wheat flour
2 T. butter
1 ½ cup milk
½ tsp. Dry mustard
½ tsp. Soy sauce
2 c. shredded Cheddar cheese

Combine vegetables, water, salt and parsley in soup kettle. Bring to a boil, cover and simmer until cauliflower is tender, approx.15-20 minutes. Knead flour into butter to form a smooth mass. Drop by bits into simmering soup and stir until smooth and slightly thickened. Gradually stir milk into soup, then add mustard and soy sauce. Heat through. Add cheese in stages, stirring to melt. Makes 2 quarts, serving 6.

Aunt Harriet's Mystery Soup

(In my memory, Aunt Harriet didn't do much cooking. She did make this soup for us once though and contributed this recipe.)

2 cans cream of chicken soup
2 cans bouillon
1 medium jar of applesauce
Curry powder to taste

Combine all ingredients and simmer. Make in the a.m. Chill. Reheat just before serving. Can be served hot or chilled. Serves about 8 ladies for lunch, according to Harriet.

4

SALADS AND SIDE DISHES

Salad Dressings:

French Dressing (Yield: 1 ½ quarts**)**

This makes a nice holiday gift. It is delicious over just plain lettuce.

> 1 pkg. MCP dry pectin
> 1 tsp. Paprika
> 2 tsp. Salt
> ½ tsp. Pepper
> ¼ c. sugar
> 1 Tbsp. Dry mustard

Add: 1 can tomato soup (Campbell's)
> 1 soup can of vinegar
> 1 tsp. Worcestershire sauce
> 1 finely minced onion and 1 clove garlic (Optional)

Then add 1 ½ cups Wesson oil a little at a time while beating after each addition.

Poppyseed Dressing – another of my favorite gift salad dressings

1 ½ c. sugar
2 tsp. Dry mustard
2 tsp. Salt
2/3 cup vinegar
2 Tbsps. onion juice

Thoroughly mix the above ingredients and then slowly add:
  1 cups salad oil

Beat until thick. Beat five minutes longer. Add 3 Tbsp. poppy seeds and beat even longer. Refrigerate.

Jet Fuel Dressing

½ tsp. Salt
½ cup red wine vinegar
¼ tsp. freshly ground black pepper
1 Tbsp. Sugar
2 cloves garlic, minced
2 tsp. Worcestershire sauce
1 Tbsp. Dijon mustard
1 Tbsp. Fresh lemon juice
1 cup water

Combine and refrigerate. Makes 2 cups.

Variations:
Italian: Add 1 tbsp. Each of fresh oregano, basil and tarragon, finely chopped or 1 tsp. Each of the same dried, crushing them first.
Asian: Add 1 tsp. Curry powder and 1/8 tsp. Dry ginger.
Mexican: add 1 tsp. Dry cumin
Tarragon: add 3 Tbsp. Fresh tarragon, finely chopped, or 1 tsp. Dried, crushed.

Caper Dressing (This tasty dressing can literally turn a simple piece of grilled fish or a skinless chicken breast into gourmet fare; also great on green, grain or vegetable salads.)

¼ cup rice vinegar
¼ tsp. Salt
¼ tsp. freshly ground pepper
1 shallot, finely chopped
1 Tbsp. Capers, drained and chopped
1 tsp. Dijon mustard
½ cup water
2 Tbsp. Salad oil

Makes 1 cup. Each 2 Tbsp. contains approximately 34 calories.

Cucumber Soup/Salad – a wonderful summer refresher

Cube one or two fresh cucumbers after you've seeded them a bit and soaked them in salt water. Add to plain yogurt with mashed fresh garlic and fresh dill, a bit of salt to taste. Refrigerate for an hour or so for best flavor. Serve as cold soup or as salad. Great in pita bread.

Phyllis Diller Potato Salad

4 large potatoes, cooked and sliced thinly
1 large white onion, slivered or finely diced
1 ½ c. mayonnaise (I often use ½ mayo/1/2 Greek yogurt)
½ - ¼ c. lemon juice
1 ½ tsp. Sugar or Splenda (sugar subst.)
Dash vinegar
Salt
Note: Do not add pepper!!!

Raw Broccoli Salad (This is always very popular at buffets or potlucks.)

   2 large bunches of broccoli, chopped
1 white or Bermuda onion, chopped

Mix the following and pour over vegetables:
1 cup mayonnaise
   1/3 cup sugar
2 T. vinegar

Cut up and fry until crisp ten slices bacon. Add bacon bits, 1 cup raisins or dried cranberries, and some unsalted sunflower seeds just before serving.

Greek Bean Salad

Dressing: ¼ c. red wine vinegar   3 T. olive oil
          ½ tsp. Dill
          ½ tsp. Basil
          ¼ tsp. Oregano
          Black pepper to taste
          ¼ c. chopped parsley
Chop and add to 12 oz. Garbanzo beans the following:
   1 medium green bell pepper
   1 medium tomato
   ½ red onion
Add 1 cup feta cheese, crumbled
   ¼ c. sliced stuffed green olives
Marinate in dressing for four hours +/-
Serve as salad on bed of lettuce…or in pita bread.

Strawberry Jell-O Salad

2 pkgs. Strawberry jello
2 cups boiling water
2 pkgs. Frozen strawberries
2 cups crushed pineapple
2 sliced bananas

Mix above ingredients and pour **half** into 9 x 13 in, pan. Chill until firm. Spread 1 small carton sour cream over top and add rest of jello mixture.

Peach, Papaya, Tomato Chile Salad

(I like to serve this with Potatoes Rosti)

4 peaches, diced
½ papaya, diced
1 T. lemon juice
2 tomatoes, cut into 8 wedges each
8 scallions, chopped
½ tsp. Jalapeno
2 Tbsp. Seasoned rice vinegar

Cucumber Salad/Soup

2 cups cubed, peeled cucumber
1 ½ tsp. salt.

After it has drained a bit, stir in:

2 cups plain yoghurt
1 clove garlic, minced
1 T. white wine vinegar
¼ tsp. dried dill weed
1 T. olive oil
1 T. scallions, chopped

Serve with fresh mint and/or seedless grapes **Ramen Salad**

Break up 2 packages of Ramen (any kind) into pan. Add seasoning packet and ½ stick margarine or butter. Heat until melted.

Add 1/4 c. Toasted sesame seeds (watch these carefully as you toast them in a pan on stove as they will brown and BURN very quickly.)

1 package of slivered almonds
½ c, toasted sunflower seeds
1 to 2 bags coleslaw (or one small head of cabbage finely grated)

Just before serving add dressing made of:

½ c. oil
¼ c. red wine vinegar
2 Tbsp. Soy sauce
¼ c. sugar

Side Dishes

Braised Cabbage with Caraway

1 1/2 # green cabbage, sliced into wedges
1 Tbsp. Minced fresh parsley
1 tsp. Sugar
Fresh ground black pepper
½ c. chicken or vegetable stock
Caraway seeds to taste (optional)

Place all but the caraway seeds in a large skillet. Cover and cook over moderate heat for 12 minutes basting several times with pan juices. When cabbage is nearly done, sprinkle it with caraway seeds. Serve with a little of the pan juices.

Potatoes Rosti

Combine the following grated potatoes and minced onions and put in colander to **drain** before adding them to the flour and eggs, below:

3 baking potatoes (3 ½ c. grated potatoes)
1/2 cup minced onions
2 T. flour
2 large eggs, beaten, or 1/2 c. Eggbeaters
In a 10-inch non-stick pan, a bit of Pam or a bit of oil, add mixture and spread evenly. Pat down firmly. Cook for 10 minutes. Invert on baking sheet or plate. Slide Rosti back into pan carefully with browned side up. Cook for 10 minutes longer. Will now be browned on both sides. Serves as a potato side dish or with *Peach, Papaya, and Tomato Chili Salad* as a luncheon or light supper entrée.

Oven-Fried French Fries

5 potatoes (sweet and/or white)
2 egg whites

Cut potatoes into favorite shapes. Dip in egg whites and sprinkle with 1 T. Cajun spices. Bake in 400 degree oven for about 40 minutes or until crisp. Check often to see how they're doing.

Cajun Spices: (Store in a covered spice jar.)

3 Tbsp. Paprika	2 tsp. cayenne
2 tsp. Onion Powder	1 tsp. oregano
2 tsp. Black Pepper	1 tsp. thyme
2 tsp. White pepper	½ tsp. Celery seed

Eggplant and Tomato Gratin

1# eggplant, sliced diagonally
1/4 cup vegetable or chicken broth
2 cloves garlic, minced
1 T. balsamic vinegar
½ tsp. Salt
½ tsp. Pepper
1 T + 1 tsp. Olive oil
1 tomato, sliced thinly
¼ c. julienned basil leaves
4 Tbsp. Bread crumbs
2 T. Parmesan or Asiago cheese
About 1/2 # turkey Italian sausage (optional)
½ large onion, minced

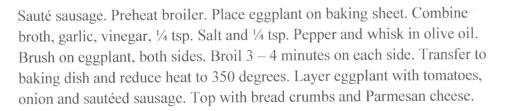

Sauté sausage. Preheat broiler. Place eggplant on baking sheet. Combine broth, garlic, vinegar, ¼ tsp. Salt and ¼ tsp. Pepper and whisk in olive oil. Brush on eggplant, both sides. Broil 3 – 4 minutes on each side. Transfer to baking dish and reduce heat to 350 degrees. Layer eggplant with tomatoes, onion and sautéed sausage. Top with bread crumbs and Parmesan cheese.

Bake 15 –20 minutes. Garnish with fresh basil. Makes 2 – 3 servings.

Cheesy Au Gratin Potatoes

Potatoes:

3 tablespoons butter	1 large onion, chopped
1/4 cup all-purpose flour	1 1/2 cups low-sodium chicken broth
1 cup milk	1 ½ teaspoons salt
1/2 teaspoon pepper	1/2 teaspoon dried thyme

8 oz. shredded cheddar cheese   26-ounce bag frozen shredded hash browns
1/2 cup light sour cream

Topping:
2 cups saltines, lightly crushed   2 tablespoons butter, melted

Melt the butter in a large pot over medium heat. Add the onion and cook until the onion is softened and translucent, about 5-6 minutes. Stir in the flour and cook, stirring constantly, for about a minute. Combine the chicken broth and milk in a liquid measure and slowly whisk in the mixture. Add the salt, pepper and thyme. Stir to combine. Bring the mixture to a boil and then reduce the heat to medium-low and simmer, stirring frequently, until the mixture is slightly thickened, about 5 minutes.

Take the pot off the heat and stir in the cheese until smooth. Mix in the frozen hash browns, lifting and folding the mixture until well combined. Finally, stir in the sour cream.

In a medium bowl, toss the lightly crushed saltines with the butter until evenly combined. Scoop out the potato mixture into a 9X13-inch baking dish and top with the buttered saltiness. If baking the potatoes by themselves, bake at 350 degrees for 45 minutes, until hot and bubbly around the edges. If baking the potatoes with a ham (my ham recipe bakes at 300 degrees), bake the potatoes for 90 minutes at 300 degrees then crank the oven to 400 degrees and bake the potatoes for 10 minutes more. In both baking situations, let the potatoes rest for 10 minutes before serving.

Pearls and Rubies – Nice holiday dish to accompany turkey fixin's.

1 ½ pounds pearl onions

Drop the unpeeled onions into boiling water to cover for about two minutes. Drain and rinse under cold water to cool. Slice off the root end and slip; off outer skins. Preheat oven to 400 degrees.

1 Tbsp. Butter or margarine

¼ c. sugar
¼ tsp. Salt
¼ tsp. freshly ground pepper
1 cup fresh cranberries
½ c. chicken stock

Heat butter in non-stick surface skillet. Add onions and cook them in single layer until they are lightly browned, shaking pan occasionally to brown evenly. Sprinkle in the sugar, salt, pepper and add the cranberries, tossing ingredients to combine. Add broth. Transfer to ceramic baking dish. Place in hot oven and bake uncovered for about 30 minutes.

Cauliflower-Broccoli Tree *(This is very pretty on a holiday buffet table.)*

Divide broccoli and cauliflower into florets. Blanch 3-4 minutes and then shock in ice water. Drain.

In a buttered round bowl of appropriate size to hold all of the cauliflower and broccoli up to about an inch above the rim of the bowl, arrange the florets – use your creative talents here to make an attractive display, a circle of each, with the stems facing toward the center, florets to the bottom and sides of bowl. Put plastic wrap over the top and weight down with something to compress. Compress overnight.

Serve with a lemon butter sauce (1/2 c. butter, 2 tbsp. lemon juice, parsley, salt & pepper, or with your favorite dip for vegetables.

5

MEAT AND POULTRY

Mark's Asian Barbecue Sauce – The Best! Well worth the effort!

¼ cup catsup (Simmer in pan until it has almost caramelized before adding:
One 12-0z. can Coke
32 oz. Can Dole pineapple juice

Simmer and reduce.
Then add 3" hunk of ginger, minced finely
½ head of garlic, mashed and minced
1 jalapeno pepper, seeded and minced
1 tsp. Dry mustard
½ tsp. Each oregano, thyme, tarragon
1 Tbsp. Chili powder
¼ c. brown sugar
½ cup cider vinegar
½ cup soy sauce

Reduce to about 2 cups. Great slathered on chicken during last few minutes of grilling.

Eye of Round Roast (or Lobster Roast)

(Ed calls this lobster roast because of the smell of melting butter, I think.)

In pan suitable for oven roasting, brown evenly on all sides an eye of round roast in 1 cube of butter. (It MUST be butter!)

Pour 1 cup dry white wine around roast. Bake for one hour in a 350 degree oven, adding more wine as needed oven roasting pan,

Add some Parmesan cheese to the wine juices and serve over sliced meat.

Garlic Egg Chicken

1/4 cup beaten eggs
3 cloves garlic

Marinate chicken breasts for up to four hours in the above mixture.

Coat with the following mixture:
> ¼ c. Parmesan or Asiago cheese, grated
> 1 ½ t. garlic powder
> 1 ½ t. parsley, finely chopped
> Salt
> Pepper
> Bread crumbs made from 2 slices light wheat bread

Spray coated crumbs with ICBNB or light butter, melted
Bake at 400 degrees for 15 minutes on each side.

Balsamic Chicken (Serves 4)

2 tsp vegetable oil

3 tbsps. balsamic vinegar

2 tsp Dijon mustard

1 large garlic clove(s), crushed

1 pound boneless, skinless chicken breast(s), four 4 oz. pieces

2 cup(s) mushroom(s), small, halved

1/3 cup(s) chicken broth

1/4 tsp dried thyme, crumbled

 Instructions

1. In a nonstick skillet, heat 1 teaspoon of oil.

2. In a medium bowl, mix 2 tablespoons of vinegar, the mustard and garlic. Add chicken and turn to coat.   3. Transfer chicken and marinade to skillet. Sauté chicken until cooked through, about 3 minutes on each side. Transfer chicken to a platter and keep warm.   4. Heat remaining teaspoon of oil in skillet. Sauté mushrooms for 1 minute. Add broth, thyme and remaining tablespoon of vinegar. Cook, stirring occasionally, until mushrooms are deep brown, about 2 minutes longer.

Grilled Chicken Breast with Tomato Nectarine Relish (or not!)

(The sweet-tart relish is a breeze to make and it really brings out the flavors of the chicken. It is also delicious with grilled tuna or swordfish steaks.)

Chicken:
1 Tbsp. Grated lemon rind
2 tsp. Olive oil
1 cloves garlic
½ tsp. Salt
Freshly ground pepper
4 (4 oz. Skinless boneless chicken breast halves

Relish:
1 cup diced tomatoes (ripe ones)
1 nectarine, pitted and diced
1 Tbsp. Chopped basil
2 tsps. Sugar
1 tsp. Grated lemon rind
1 tsp. Balsamic or cider vinegar
¼ tsp. Salt
Freshly ground pepper

Combine the chicken ingredients in a zip-lock bag and add chicken. Refrigerate and marinate for a couple of hours or more. Prepare the grill. Meanwhile, combine the relish ingredients and set aside. Pour off and discard the marinade. Grill the chicken, turning once, until cooked through and no longer pink in center…about 10 minutes. Serve immediately with the relish. (I use the George Foreman grill for this…delicious!)
A variation for the relish: cucumbers and Kalamata olives for the nectarine; mango or papaya with some jalapeno peppers work well, too.)

Broiled Leg of Lamb – in half an hour!

Have the butcher bone a leg of lamb…and butterfly it out as flat as possible. Rub down with garlic and soy sauce. Let marinate in refrigerator for 2 hours.

Broil ten minutes on skin side. Then broil10 minutes on other side. Let set for another 10 minutes in OFF oven. Slice thinly and serve with mint sauce or jelly. Delicious! And so impressive to guests who know that you worked all day and then could prepare this amazing entrée.

Leg 'o Lamb the more traditional way

Cut slits all over the leg of lamb with bone in. Bury two whole heads of garlic in these little slits. Rub salt, pepper, parsley, paprika with fresh rosemary all over the lamb. Brown in high oven (400 degrees). Turn and brown other side. Quarter 3 – 4 large onions and surround lamb with them.
Pour two cups of red wine over all…and reduce heat to 350 degrees. Cook slowly until done, adding water periodically, as needed...

Lamb Hip Steak with Vegetables (This was one of our Berkeley student poor-man meals during graduate school.)

In large sheet of foil – per serving:

1 lamb him steak	4 slices potato
3/4 inch slice of eggplant	Thick slice of tomato
Thinly sliced onion	Parsley
Basil	1 Tbsp. bottled French dressing
1 T. sherry	

Bake for three hours at 300 degrees. Serve in the little packets with some good French bread to sop up the juices.

French Lamb Stew

2# lean stewing lamb, cut into 1" cubes
3 T. olive oil or salad oil (I usually reduce the amount of oil)
1 medium onion, chopped
1 clove garlic, minced
2 T. flour
1 ½ c. chicken broth
1 ½ tsp. Salt
1 bay leaf, crumbled
¼ tsp. Marjoram
2 T. lemon juice (or ½ c. dry white wine)
6-8 small white onions
3 carrots, scraped and sliced
3 medium potatoes, cut into pieces
1 T. finely chopped parsley

Heat oil in heavy 4 qt. Kettle. Brown meat on all sides. Remove and sauté onion and garlic. Return meat and sprinkle with flour. Add broth and seasoning. Mix well. Cover and simmer ½ hour. Add white onions and simmer 15 minutes. Add carrots and potatoes. Simmer 20 minutes until just fork tender. Add parsley and serve with French bread and a green salad.

Saté

(Valerie learned this from the mother of a Dutch/Indonesian junior high school friend in Marin County years ago.) It is a real treat served with lumpia and rice, but we always enjoy it with potato salad when we don't have time or energy for making lumpia, which tends to be quite time consuming.

Marinade: (This is excellent marinade for almost everything.)

2 cloves garlic, minced
Juice of one lemon
4 T. soy sauce
1 T. maple syrup
1 T. oil

Marinate 2 ½ pounds sirloin steak, tri-tips, or boneless cross-rib roast cut into 1" cubes for several minutes to several hours, depending on your time schedule. Put on wooden skewers that have been well soaked in water. Grill to desired doneness.

Lumpia (Indonesian egg rolls)

Egg roll skins
Tofu

Brown 1 onion, chopped   1 clove garlic, minced
Salt and pepper   tiny bit of ginger, crushed
1/2 # ground chuck
Add: ½ can bamboo shoots, sliced
     ¼ # snow peas
     ½ bunch green onions, sliced
     Candied melon, 1 piece, sliced (optional)

Fry four pieces of tofu, cubed. Add to above mixture with one bag of bean sprouts. Heat through. Stuff egg roll skins, creating egg roll shaped packages. Use egg white to make skin stick to itself. Deep fat fry until crisp and lightly browned. Drain on paper towels before serving hot.

London Broil

Marinate 2 ½ # flank steak in the following for at least three hours:

   1 clove garlic, minced   1 c. oil
   ½ c. vinegar   1 tsp. salt
   ¼ tsp. Pepper   2 tsp. Dry mustard
   2 tsp. Worcestershire sauce
   Dash cayenne

Broil or grill on hot fire three to four minutes on each side. Carve diagonally across grain into thin slices. (You may refrigerate and reuse the marinade for meat, fish or poultry, but do not reuse after using it for fish or poultry.)

Roast Chicken with Grapes

(Valerie made this as a teenager after seeing it on the cover of Sunset Magazine. It continues to be one of my favorites.)

Rub outside of whole chicken with ½ cut lemon. Mix 2 Tbsp. Lemon juice with 2 T. whipping cream and spoon inside cavity of chicken.

Bake at 375 degrees for about 1 ½ hours. Baste with whipping cream (1/2 cup) last 45 minutes. Add rest of cream to pan. Sauté 1 ½ c. to 2 c. Thompson seedless grapes in butter. Serve around chicken with sauce in gravy boat.

Chicken Cacciatore

4-5 # chicken
3 Tbsp. Olive oil
1 large onion
3 cloves garlic, minced
1 rib celery, diced
1 can tomato sauce
½ c. red wine, optional

1 can Italian pack peeled tomatoes
1 bell pepper, diced
1 tsp. Salt
¼ tsp. Pepper
½ tsp. Oregano or Italian seasoning

Cut chicken into serving pieces, rinse, and dry. Sauté chicken in olive oil until nicely browned. Add onion and garlic and brown lightly. Add celery, tomato sauce, tomatoes, and seasoning. Simmer slowly for 45 minutes to one hour. Add wine 15 minutes before serving. Serve over spaghetti. Serves 4 – 6.

Oven Fried Chicken

1 ½ c. buttermilk pancake mix (Krusteaz) 1 tsp. salt
½ tsp. pepper
3 Tbsp. dried onion flakes or diced onion
Cut up chicken
1 cube butter

 Mix first five ingredients. Dredge chicken pieces in mixture. Sprinkle remaining over top in baking dish. Drizzle melted butter over all and bake at 350 degrees for about 1 1 ½ hours.

No-Burn Chicken Barbecue Marinade/Sauce (my favorite)

(This is enough for 10 broiler halves – you can make ahead and just pour out what is needed over the chicken you are cooking that day. Do not save, however, any that has been contaminated by raw chicken.) Baste halves each time you turn the chicken pieces. I actually marinate them and then baste only occasionally.

Beat: 1 egg
          1 cup oil

Add and stir: 1 pt. Cider vinegar
                    3 T. salt
                    1 T. poultry seasoning
                    1 tsp. Ground pepper

Marinated Chicken Breasts for Salad

(This is an excellent luncheon entrée – arranged on mixed greens with cherry tomatoes or grapes, etc.]

Remove the skin form 6 whole chicken breasts and simmer in 2 cups water with ½ tsp. Salt until all pink color disappears – about 12 minutes. Drain chicken and chill. Remove chicken carefully from bones. Arrange in bowl. Combine the following ingredients and pour over chicken. Cover and refrigerate for at least six hours or overnight.

1 cup salad oil   1/3 cup tarragon wine vinegar
1 tsp. Salt   ½ tsp each .garlic salt
                                       and seasoned salt

1 green onion, finely chopped   ¼ c. finely chopped parsley Sprinkle
with 2 T. finely chopped parsley.

Sandabs, Rex Sole, Trout Meniere

¼ c. flour	½ tsp. Salt
4 small fish	pepper
½ c. butter	1 T. chopped parsley
¼ tsp. Dried tarragon leaves	2 T. lemon juice
1 tsp. grated lemon zest	

Mix flour and ½ tsp. Salt. Sprinkle inside of fish with salt and pepper. Thoroughly coat fish with flour and salt mixture. Melt half of the butter in skillet over moderate heat. Add fish and brown well, about five minutes on each side. Remove to warm platter. Add the remaining ¼ cup butter, parsley, tarragon, lemon juice and zest. Heat until butter foams. Serve over trout. Serves 4.

Shrimp with Capers and Dill

[I got this from a Greek friend. It may be served with some pilaf, polenta, quinoa, or angel hair pasta with a spring greens salad or just with sliced baguette as an appetizer. It's quite satisfying as either.]

Serves 4

¼ cup extra virgin olive oil
1 lb. shrimp, raw, peeled and deveined
3 Tbsp. fresh lemon juice
2 tsp. Dijon mustard
2 Tbsp. fresh dill, chopped
2 cloves garlic, minced
The green part of 2 scallions, chopped
1 Tbsp. chopped fresh parsley
1 Tbsp. grated lemon zest
2 Tbsp. capers, rinsed Splash
  of wine (optional) Salt and
  Pepper to taste.

In a bowl mix the olive oil, the herbs, capers, mustard and stir until blended. Adjust flavoring to your taste with salt and pepper.

In a large skillet on medium high heat and with a bit of olive oil, add lightly seasoned shrimp. Saute just until pink. Remove with slotted spoon. Deglaze pan with splash of wine. After you've loosened up any brown bits, add shrimp back in along with the caper dill sauce. Reduce heat and stir to warm sauce through and finish cooking shrimp, but not too much.

Serve warm or at room temperature as an appetizer, sprinkled with fresh dill on top, with a slice of lemon, crusty bread and a fruity wine to hold up to the acidity of the sauce.

Salmon Bake with Pecan Crunch Coating

2 Tbsp. Dijon mustard
2 Tbsp. Melted butter
4 tsp. Honey
¼ c. fresh bread crumbs ¼ c. finely chopped
pecans   or walnuts
2 tsp. Chopped parsley
4 – 4oz. Alaska salmon fillets
      (4-6 oz. Each)
Salt and pepper
Lemon wedges

Baking time: 10 minutes per inch thickness in 450 degree oven.

Mix together mustard, butter and honey in a small bowl; set aside. Mix together bread crumbs, pecans and parsley in another small bowl; set aside.
Season each salmon fillet with salt and pepper. Place on a lightly oiled baking dish or broiling pan. Brush each fillet with mustard/honey mixture. Pat top of each fillet with bread crumb mixture. Bake until salmon just flakes when tested with a fork.

6
THE DISH THAT HAS EVERYTHING

Wild Rice and Shrimp Casserole

(An excellent side dish for a ham dinner…or to take to a potluck.)

Cook according to package directions:
   1 package of Uncle Ben's wild rice mixture
   1 package Rice-a-Roni or 1 cup white rice and 1 cup wild rice

Sauté 1# mushrooms
1 cup chopped onion
2 cups celery
1 green pepper

Add 1# fresh shrimp, peeled, deveined and chopped and continue cooking until shrimp are just barely cooked. Add: ½ cup slivered almonds +/- 2 cans cream of mushroom soup…or enough to moisten

Top with shredded cheddar cheese. May be refrigerated until just before ready to heat and serve. Heat through.

I sometimes add red bell pepper, water chestnuts…use your imagination.

Serves 12 generously as side dish for dinner; 20 ladies for luncheon!

Cheese Soufflé

(Don't be afraid to try this...soufflé's are not difficult. You just want to have the table set and the salad on while it's baking as, of course, it will deflate soon after you take it out of the oven.)

¼ c. butter	1/4 c. flour
¼ tsp.salt	Dash cayenne
1 cup milk	
2 c. shredded cheddar cheese	
¼ c. grated Parmesan cheese	5 eggs, separated

Melt butter, whisk in flour, salt, cayenne; add milk and cook, stirring constantly until it thickens. Stir in cheese until melted.

Remove from heat. Add small amount of sauce to lightly beaten egg yolk mixture to temper it. Then the tempered eggs to rest of white sauce.

Beat egg whites until stiff, but not dry. Fold into sauce. Pour into ungreased 1 ½ qt. Soufflé dish. Bake at 350 degrees for 40 minutes. Serves 4.

For seafood soufflé: Add 1 cup diced cooked crab, shrimp, or lobster or combination thereof to cheese/egg yolk mix before folding in the whites.

For mushroom soufflé: 1 c. sautéed mushrooms

For ham soufflé: ½ to ¾ c. finely chopped ham.

Moussaka

Cook two large potatoes. Cool and dice. Place in bottom of 9 x 13" pan. Slice eggplant. Dip lightly (or spray) in oil and bake at 400 degrees until well done. Cut into large dice.

Combine the following and add to eggplant:
   2# ground beef or combination of lamb and pork.
Sauté and add: 1 finely diced onion   ½ # mushrooms.
Add ½ - 1 cup breadcrumbs
1 minced clove garlic
2 T. chopped parsley
      1-2 eggs, lightly beaten
      ¾ c. catsup
      ¼ tsp. Nutmeg
      ¼ tsp. Cinnamon
       Salt and pepper to taste

Layer over potatoes in baking dish.
Top with the following custard:
Melt: ¼ c. butter Stir in and
whisk well:
   2 T. flour
Gradually add, while stirring constantly:
   2 c. milk

Add one third of thickened sauce to 3 beaten eggs to temper the eggs…and then add the egg mixture to the remaining sauce. Cook for one minutes more. Pour over the moussaka mixture in baking dish. Sprinkle with Parmesan cheese. Bake 30 minutes (50 minutes if it has been refrigerated).

Laurie's Prize-Winning Meatless Moussaka

(Laurie Snodgrass won 1st prize in Vegetarian entrees at Davis Enterprise Cooking Contest)

4# eggplant, cut in rounds, oiled and broiled
Custard;

2 Tbsp. butter

1 ½ milk

White pepper

2 c. ricotta cheese

1/4 c. flour

grated nutmeg

4 large eggs, beaten

Melt butter, add flour. Stir for about three minutes. Remove from heat and add milk, whisking until smooth. Season. Add ricotta cheese and eggs to milk sauce.

Tomato Sauce:

2 c. minced onion
2 cloves garlic, minced
2# tin tomatoes, drained and chopped
1 T. tomato paste
1 tsp. salt
¾ tsp. Cinnamon
¼ tsp. Allspice
¼ tsp. Oregano

Sauté onion and garlic with a bit of oil. Add tomato paste and tomatoes, seasoning. Simmer over low heat for 25 minutes.
Spread one-half of sauce in bottom of pan. Top with half of eggplant. Sprinkle with Parmesan cheese. Add remaining sauce, eggplant. Then spoon custard over all…and sprinkle with Parmesan. Garnish with broiled tomato slices and parsley.

Baked Macaroni and Cheese

(Page 355 of my Good Housekeeping cookbook, which I received as a wedding present in 1951 is scotch taped and all but worn out. It is without doubt the best macaroni and cheese I've ever eaten! This was Valerie's specialty from the time she was 12 years old. Her macaroni and cheese far surpassed mine because, unfortunately, I never followed a real recipe...just made a white sauce and threw some cheese in. Valerie, a scientist at heart, follows recipes exactly...and this one is superb! Try it. You'll like it!)

½ # cheddar cheese (2 c. grated)	speck pepper
2 c. raw macaroni	2 cups milk
4 tsp. Minced onion	1 Tbsp. flour
2 T. butter + 4 tsp. butter	1/4 tsp. Dry mustard
3/4 tsp. Salt	3/4 c. soda crackers

1. In large kettle, put on to boil 2 quarts water with ¾ tsp. Salt.

2. Fill base of double boiler with about 2" water; put top in place, cover and bring water to boil.

3. Heat oven to 400 degrees. Thoroughly grease a 1 ½ qt. Casserole dish.

4. With medium grater, grate cheese.

5. Boil macaroni, uncovered until done.

6. Mince onion, put in double boiler with 2 Tbsp. Butter. When butter is melted, stir in next four ingredients. Slowly stir in milk; cook over boiling water until smooth and hot, stirring often. When macaroni is tender, drain into colander. Turn into casserole.

7. To smooth sauce, add ¾ of grated cheese; stir until cheese is melted.

8. Now melt 4 tsp. Butter in small saucepan. (Using rolling pin or Cuisinart, create cracker crumbs from soda crackers.)

9. Pour cheese sauce over macaroni, while tossing lightly with a fork so that all of the macaroni gets nicely coated.

10. Sprinkle remaining cheese over top. Toss cracker crumbs into melted butter, coating evenly. Sprinkle over cheese.

11. Bake in 400 degree oven for 20 minutes.

Serves 4
Baked Beans the Easy Way

6 slices bacon, cut up   1/3 c. onion, chopped
1 50-oz. can B & M baked beans
1 small can crushed pineapple with juice
1/3 c. catsup   1/2 cup. brown sugar
2 T. mustard   2 tsp. Worcestershire sauce

Fry bacon and brown onions in same pan, pouring off all the oil when done. Combine all ingredients in 2 qt. Casserole or bean pot if you really want to fool everyone into thinking these are the real thing! Bake uncovered for one hour in 350 degree oven, stirring occasionally.

Manicotti

1 c. chopped onions   2 tsp. Oregano
2# fresh spinach   ½ tsp. Dill weed
2 c. mashed tofu   1 tsp. Basil
¼ c. whole wheat flour   8 c. marinara sauce
1 T. low sodium soy sauce   Manicotti shells (14)

Sauté onion in ½ c. water for five minutes. Add chopped spinach and sauté until limp. Add tofu, soy sauce, oregano, basil and dill weed. (You can add Parmesan for richer flavor.) Stir in flour. Mix and set aside.Put a layer of marinara sauce in bottom of baking dish. Stuff mixture into manicotti shells…or you can use layers of lasagna noodles. Will fill 14 manicotti shells. Top with more sauce and bake at 350 degrees for 45 minutes.

Meat Loaf with Brown Sugar–Ketchup Glaze

If you like, you can omit the bacon topping from the loaf. In this case, brush on half of the glaze before baking and the other half during the last 15 minutes of baking. I recommend the standard meat loaf mix of equal parts beef, pork, and veal, available at most grocery stores.

Brown Sugar-Ketchup Glaze

> 1/2 cup ketchup or chili sauce
> 1 Tbsp. brown sugar
> Cider vinegar to taste
> Bit of dry mustard
> (Sorry – this is one of those non-recipes. I just do it by taste!

Meat Loaf

2 teaspoons vegetable oil
1 medium onion, chopped
2 garlic cloves, minced
2 large eggs
1/2 teaspoon dried thyme leaves
1 teaspoon salt
1/2 teaspoon ground black pepper
2 teaspoons Dijon mustard
2 teaspoons Worcestershire sauce
1/4 teaspoon hot red pepper sauce
1/2 cup whole milk or plain yogurt
2 pounds meat loaf mix (equal parts lean ground chuck, ground pork, and ground   are ideal
2/3 cup crushed saltine crackers (about 16) or quick oatmeal or 1 1/3 cups fresh
Bread crumbs
1/3 cup minced fresh parsley leaves
6–8 ounces thin-sliced bacon (8 to 12 slices, depending on loaf shape) (Meat Loaf – cont'd)

1. **For the glaze**: Mix all ingredients in small saucepan; set aside.

2. **For the meat loaf**: Heat oven to 350 degrees. Heat oil in medium skillet. Add onion and garlic; sauté until softened, about 5 minutes. Set aside to cool while preparing remaining ingredients.

3. Mix eggs with thyme, salt, pepper, mustard, Worcestershire sauce, pepper sauce, and milk or yogurt. Add egg mixture to meat in large bowl along with crackers, parsley, and cooked onion and garlic; mix with fork until evenly blended and meat mixture does not stick to bowl. (If mixture sticks, add additional milk or yogurt, a couple tablespoons at a time, until mix no longer sticks.)

4. Turn meat mixture onto work surface. With wet hands, pat mixture into approximately 9 x 5-inch loaf shape. Place on foil-lined (for easy cleanup) shallow baking pan. Brush with half the glaze, then arrange bacon slices, crosswise, over loaf, overlapping slightly and tucking only bacon tip ends under loaf.

5. Bake loaf until bacon is crisp and internal temperature of loaf registers 160 degrees, about 1 hour. Cool at least 20 minutes. Simmer remaining glaze over
medium heat until thickened slightly. Slice meat loaf and serve with extra glaze passed separately.

The Best Ratatouille

1 ½# eggplant, unpeeled 1 /-
1 t. olive oil
2 large onions, thickly sliced
1 large green bell pepper, seeded and diced
1 large red bell pepper, seeded and diced
1 Tbsp. finely minced garlic
2 ½ # tomatoes (I use canned chopped tomatoes   unless fresh tomatoes are
   really ripe and good!)
1 ½# zucchini, cut into ½" slices
½ tsp. Thyme
½ tsp. Oregano
2 tsp. Minced fresh basil or ½ tsp. Dry
½ tsp. Ground pepper
¼ tsp. Salt
1/8 tsp. Cayenne (omit for children's taste buds)
2 Tbsp. Minced fresh parsley

Cut the eggplant into ¾" cubes. (If you find eggplant bitter, you can place in
colander and sprinkle with salt, weigh down with a plate or bowl and let
eggplant drain for half an hour. I usually omit this step and can't tell the
difference.) I sauté in water for the least possible amount of fat in our diet,
but you can use 1 tsp. Oil. Sauté onion and peppers until onions are
translucent. Add garlic and tomatoes. Cook vegies, stirring for about 3
minutes. Add eggplant and cook with herbs until eggplant is done.

I serve this over brown rice. This freezes well, but it is best to freeze it
without spices.

Couscous with Steamed Vegetables

Steam any combination of vegetables you like. I usually use broccoli, cauliflower, carrots, zucchini, onion, turnips or rutabagas, red potatoes, sweet potatoes, cabbage, yellow squash, or some combination thereof. Put slower cooking vegetables on bottom, zucchini on top. While vegies are steaming:

Variation #1: Sauté mushrooms, garlic and onions. Place large scoop of couscous in center of plate, surrounded by steamed vegetables. Place sautéed mushroom combination in center over couscous.

Variation #2: Omit mushrooms. Make a sauce with an apricot jam or raisins, cranberry or other kind of chutney, thinned with a bit of orange juice, a bit of fresh ginger…whatever you like…to taste.

Note: *I buy couscous in bulk at the local food co-op. It is very inexpensive there, whereas if you buy it in the small boxes at the supermarket, you may pay the price of import from France. The following is the amount I usually cook for three people:*

Bring to boil 1 c. orange juice
       ½ c. water
       2 T. fresh ginger, grated
       1 T. finely diced red onion

Pour over couscous. Cover and let set while your vegetables are steaming.

(Optional: Top with 2 T. toasted pine nuts just before serving.)

Mexican Tabbouleh

1 cup bulgur wheat
1 6 oz. Can Snappy Tom or Spicy V-8 juice
10 oz. Can beef bouillon
Heat liquid to boiling and pour over wheat.
Stir in: 1 medium cucumber, seeded, chopped and peeled
2 tomatoes, chopped
½ c. green pepper, diced
½ c. chopped parsley
¼ c. chopped scallions or red onion
1 – 2 T. cilantro or parsley
1 minced jalapeno

Make a dressing of the following:

¼ c. fresh lemon juice   cayenne or black pepper
1 tsp. Thyme   1 Tbsp. Olive oil
1 clove garlic

Chicago Style Pizza

Mix the following ingredients for 10 minutes:

2 c. tepid water
2 pkg. Quick rise yeast
½ c. salad oil
4 T. olive oil
3 c. flour
½ c. coarse cornmeal

Add 2 ½ c. more flour and knead with dough hook or by hand for 15 minutes (or until smooth and satiny). Let rise twice. Spread on two large pizza pans or cookie sheets. Bake crusts for 3 – 5 minutes at 450 degrees. Grate mozzarella and provolone cheeses and sprinkle on crusts.

Spread with pizza sauce. Slice tomatoes, diced onions, and any of your favorite toppings. Freshly grated Parmesan cheese. Bake 35 – 40 minutes at 475 degrees.

Polenta

This is a basic recipe that can be enhanced with Gorgonzola cheese, walnuts, basil or served simply for breakfast with maple syrup; grilled; or my favorite way is the gratin that follows. I buy the cornmeal in bulk at the Co-op.

6 cups water	1 ½ tsp. Salt
1 ½ c. coarse cornmeal	¼ tsp. Pepper Cayenne pepper, optional 2 T. butter
½ c. grated Parmesan or Asiago cheese (about 1 ½ oz.)	

Lightly spray a 9 x 13 inch pan with Pam and set aside. Bring the water to a rapid boil in a large saucepan. Add the salt, then vigorously whisk as you slowly pour in the cornmeal (so that it does not get lumpy). Reduce heat and cook at a low boil until quite thick – sometimes as long as 20 minutes, until grains have opened up and the polenta is smooth. Stir frequently and be careful as it can splatter if it cooks too fast.

Remove the pan from heat, stir in pepper, butter and cheese. Pour the hot polenta into the prepared pan and set aside to cool. This can be done way ahead and refrigerated until ready to use.

For the following gratin, cut into 12 squares and then each square into two triangles.

Polenta Gratin with Salsa Rojas (or tomatillo sauce)

1 T. olive oil
¾ # white mushrooms, thickly sliced
¾ tsp. Salt
4 cloves garlic, finely minced
1 med. Zucchini, diced
½ red bell pepper, diced
1 tsp. Cumin seed, toasted and ground
Cayenne pepper
1 Tbsp. chopped fresh marjoram or oregano (1 tsp. Dry)
¼ # smoked or regular mozzarella cheese
Polenta
Salsa Rojas or salsa of your choice

Make the polenta and while it cools, cook the vegetables and make the salsa Rojas, below.

Heat ½ T olive oil and sauté mushrooms over high heat with ½ tsp. Salt until golden and crisp, about five minutes. Add half the garlic and sauté for a minute more. Transfer mushrooms to bowl and set aside.

In the same pan, add rest of vegetables and remaining salt and cayenne. Sauté over medium heat for 7 minutes; add remaining garlic and sauté for another minute or so. Remove from heat and toss with mushrooms and half the fresh herbs.

Preheat oven to 375 degrees. Pour the salsa Rojas into the bottom of the 9 x 13 baking dish. Arrange the polenta triangles upright in rows across the width of the dish, overlapping them slightly; use all of the polenta. Sprinkle the vegetables between and around the triangles, separating the rows as you go. Sprinkle the grated cheese over the gratin. Cover and bake for 30 to 40 minutes, until the sauce is bubbly and the polenta is heated through. (If you use fresh marjoram, you can sprinkle it over the top just before serving.)

Salsa Rojas

½ med. Onion, chopped   1 tsp. Cumin seed, toasted and ground
 Salt   5 cloves garlic, finely chopped
1 ½ # fresh tomatoes
    or equivalent canned tomatoes

Sauté the onions in a bit of water or olive oil. Add the cumin and ½ tsp. Salt
Sauté until onions begin to release juices…add garlic and sauté until onions
are soft. Add the tomatoes and simmer over medium-low heat for 30 minutes.
(Tip: If the tomatoes are very acidic, add a little sugar to balance the flavors.)

Broccoli and Bow Ties (an absolute favorite!)

Kosher salt
8 cups Broccoli florets
1/2 #   Bow tie pasta (farfalle)
2 tbsp Unsalted butter
2 tbsps.Olive oil
1 tsp.   Minced garlic
Zest of one lemon
1/2 tsp.Freshly ground black pepper
1   tbsp Freshly squeezed lemon juice
1/4 cup Toasted pignoli (pine) nuts
1/2 cup Parmesan cheese
1 can Artichoke hearts -- (optional – just for variety's sake)

Bring large quantity of water to a boil Cook the bowtie pasta according to package directions – about 12 minutes. About three minutes before pasta is done, add broccoli to the cooking pasta. Drain pasta and broccoli and add to sauce that has been made as follows:

Meanwhile, in a small sauté pan, heat the butter and oil and cook the garlic and lemon zest over medium-low heat for 1 minute. Off the heat, add salt and pepper to taste, as well as lemon juice.

Toss well. Season to taste, sprinkle with the pignolis and cheese, if using, and serve.

To toast pignolis, place them in a dry sauté pan over medium-low heat and cook, tossing often, for about 5 minutes, until light brown.

7
WHAT EVERYBODY KNEADS

The Bread the Snodgrass Kids Grew Up On

1 cake yeast   2 c. lukewarm water

2 Tbsp. Granulated sugar   2 tsp. Salt

3 c. white flour   ½ c. hot water

 ½ c. brown sugar   2 Tbsp. Shortening

 3 cups +/- whole wheat flour

Soften yeast in lukewarm water. Add granulated sugar, salt and white flour in that order. Beat until smooth; set in warm place until light and bubbly. This is called "proofing the yeast." If it doesn't get light and bubbly, your yeast may not be active. You'll need to start over with fresh yeast.

Combine hot water with brown sugar and shortening. Cool until lukewarm; then add to sponge. Add the whole wheat flour, mix smooth, knead and let rise. Mold into two loaves. Place in greased loaf pans. Let rise until doubled in bulk. Bake at 375 degrees for 50 minutes. Take out of pans and let cool on rack before slicing.

Joan's Favorite Italian Bread

3 cups warm water
1 Tablespoon yeast
1/2 teaspoon sugar
1 Tablespoon salt
8 cups flour -- (6-8 cups)

Dissolve sugar in the water and then sprinkle in the yeast. Add 1 cup flour...and then let stand for half an hour or so to proof yeast. Add salt and 3 cups of flour and beat until smooth. (I used Kitchen Aid with dough hook in my later years.) The more you beat at this point, the lighter the bread will be. Add in enough flour to make stiff dough. Turn out onto floured board and knead until smooth and soft.

Oil a good sized bowl and turn bread into it...and then over, so that oiled side is up. Cover with towel or plastic wrap and let rise until doubled in bulk in a warm spot...sunny window.

When doubled (couple of hours probably, depending on heat in your kitchen) punch down and knead briefly in bowl. Let rise again until doubled in bulk (this will be shorter time – an hour perhaps. Preheat oven to 450 degrees. Meanwhile knead gently and shape dough into two long loaves or three football-shaped loaves. Place on a large lightly greased baking sheet (I use a double Italian loaf pan which I got from King Arthur's Flour). Sprinkle with sesame seeds. Score bread with a sharp knife very lightly and mist bread with water before placing in oven. Mist several times until bread is golden brown and sounds hollow when tapped on bottom...about 40-45 minutes.

Let cool on rack before slicing.

Thirty Minute Rolls

1 cup plus 2 Tbsps. warm water
1/3 C oil
2 Tbsps. yeast
1/4 C sugar
1/2 tsp salt
1 egg
3 1/2 C flour

Heat oven to 400 degrees.

In your mixer bowl combine the water, oil, yeast and sugar and allow it to rest for 10 minutes. Using your dough hook, mix in the salt, egg and flour. Knead with hook until will incorporated and dough is soft and smooth. (Just a few minutes)

Form dough into 12 balls and then place in a greased 9 x 13 pan and allow to rest for 10 minutes. Bake for 10 minutes at 400 degrees or until golden brown.

Focaccia

Combine 4 ½ tsp. Yeast with ½ c. warm water and 1 Tbsp. Sugar in a large bowl. Let it stand for ten minutes to proof the yeast. It should be foamy after ten minutes or so. Add: ½ c. extra virgin olive oil and 1 ½ c. warm water.

Add to the wet mixture:

5 ½ c. unbleached white flour   2 tsp. Salt

2 Tbsp. Fresh rosemary, 3 Tbsp. Fresh sage, OR 3 Tbsp. Mixed chopped herbs

It may be necessary to knead in the last of the flour. Knead vigorously for five to ten minutes. Add a little more flour if necessary to keep it from being too sticky. Place dough in oiled bowl, turn to coat surface. Cover with plastic wrap or damp towel, and allow it to rise for 1 ½ hours. I especially like it with chopped pine nuts gently pressed into the surface prior to baking – about ½ cup chopped pine nuts.

Preheat oven to 450 degrees and lightly oil with olive oil two 9 x 13 baking dishes or one large jelly roll pan for thicker sandwich focaccia. Press dough onto pans. Let rise for 30 minutes. Dimple the dough with your fingertips, brush with olive oil and sprinkle with coarse sea salt. Place in oven. Reduce temperature to 375 degrees and bake for 20-25 minutes (more for the thicker focaccia) until light golden. Transfer to rack to cool.

You can add 1/3 to ½ c. chopped drained sun-dried tomatoes to the wet ingredients for variation…and then brush with sun dried tomato oil for more intense flavor.

Combine olive oil, rosemary, salt, orange zest, and pepper. Sprinkle with roasted red peppers or tomatoes, scallions and olives. Bake. Or sautéed red onions, ½ c. chopped pitted Kalamata olives, roasted garlic, or chili-infused oil are other interesting variations.

For a delicious eggplant or portabella mushroom burger, split focaccia and treat as a hamburger bun with all the fixins!

Ciabatta

Sponge:

1/8 tsp. active dry yeast
2 tbsp. warm water
1/3 cup warm water
1 cup bread flour

Bread:

Sponge
½ tsp. active dry yeast
2 tbsp. warm milk
2/3 cup water
1 tbsp. olive oil
2 cups bread flour
1 ½ tsp. salt

1.   To Make Sponge: In a small bowl stir together 1/8 tsp. of yeast and 2 tbsp. warm water and let stand five minutes or until creamy. Add the remaining sponge ingredients and stir for four minutes. Cover bowl with plastic wrap. Let sponge stand at room temperature for at least 12 hours or up to one day.

2.   To Make the Bread: In a small bowl stir together yeast and milk and let stand five minutes or until creamy. In bowl of standing mixer fitted with dough hook blend together the milk mixture, sponge, water, oil and flour at low speed until flour is just moistened. Add salt and mix until smooth and elastic, about 8 minutes. Scrape dough into an oiled bowl and cover with plastic wrap.

3.   Let dough rise at room temperature until doubled in bulk, about 1 ½ hours. (Dough will be sticky and full of air bubbles.) Turn dough out onto a well-floured work surface and cut in half. Transfer each half to a parchment sheet and form into an irregular oval about 9 inches long. Dimple loaves with

floured fingers and dust tops with flour. Cover loaves with dampened kitchen towel. Let loaves rise at room temperature until doubled in bulk, 1 ½ to 2 hours.

4.   At least 45 minutes before baking ciabatta, put a baking stone on oven rack in lowest position in oven and preheat oven to 425 degrees.

5.   Transfer loaf on its parchment to a rimless baking sheet with a long side of loaf parallel to far edge of baking sheet. Line up far edge of baking sheet with far edge of stone, tilt baking sheet to slide loaf with parchment onto back half of stone or tiles. Transfer remaining loaf. Bake ciabatta loaves 20 minutes or until pale golden. Cool on rack before cutting.

Teedy's Biscuits

[Teedy was the nickname of my Aunt, Elora Kelso. Her real name was Elora (my middle name came from her, too.) No one ever called her that from the time my brother dubbed her Teedy, trying to say "Auntie". Teedy was my favorite adult as I was growing up...she always had time to listen. She taught me to cook when I was quite young...and to sew...and to behave! Her philosophy was that if you waited to serve a meal until everyone was half-starved and then served them a good homemade biscuit or bread along with it, they were convinced you were an exceptional cook!

And she was by far the best cook I've ever known...she could stretch two pork chops to serve 6 people or create clam fritters to die for – and did!

Cut into 3 c. Bisquick a half stick of margarine or butter.
Add milk – approximately ¾ cup.

Pat out on floured board to about ¾ inch thick. Cut rounds and dip both sides in melted butter or oil. Bake at 450 degrees until lightly browned.

Teedy's Dumplings

(These are the ones I use for blackberry dumplings. Omit the sugar if you are using them for soups or chicken and dumplings.)

2 c. flour, sifted	4 T. sugar
3 tsp. baking powder	1 ½ tsp. Salt

Milk – start with about ½ cup and add just enough for the dough to be at the consistency between muffins and biscuits.

These can be added to any boiling liquid. Cover. DON'T PEAK! For 20 minutes.

(For fruit dumplings, be sure fruit is sweet enough and that there is plenty of liquid to allow simmering for 20 minutes. Remember, you aren't allowed to peak!)

Homemade Bisquick

8 ½ c. flour	1 ½ c. instant non-fat dry milk
1 T. baking powder	2 tsp. Cream of tartar
1 T. salt	2 ¼ c. vegetable shortening
1 tsp. Soda	

Sift together dry ingredients. Blend well. With pastry blender, cut in shortening until evenly distributed. Resembles cornmeal in texture. Put in airtight container. Label. Store in cool, dry place. Use within 10 to 12 weeks. Makes about 13 cups of Bisquick.

Hush Puppies (Jean Stump)

2 c. cornmeal	1 c. buttermilk
2 heaping Tbsp. Flour	1 beaten egg
2 tsp. baking powder	1 diced onion
1 tsp. Salt	1 pinch garlic powder
½ tsp. Soda	or clove garlic, mashed

Combine dry ingredients. Add beaten egg, garlic, onion and buttermilk. Drop by spoonful into hot oil (375 degrees). Drain on paper towel. These are superb with any fried fish.

Depot Cornbread

1 c. cornmeal	1 c. flour
2 tsp. baking powder	½ tsp. Salt
5 T. sugar	2 eggs
2 T. melted shortening	1 c. milk

Mix dry ingredients. Mix eggs, shortening and milk. Combine dry and wet ingredients. Pour into buttered 4 x 8" pan and bake at 375 degrees for 55 minutes.

Challah is a special Jewish braided bread eaten on Sabbath and holidays.

Bring to a boil: 2 c. milk

8 T. butter

1/3 c. granulated sugar

Remove from heat. Pour into mixing bowl and let cool to lukewarm.

Stir in **2 packages of yeast**. Let stand for ten minutes.

Beat **4 eggs** and stir into milk mixture with **1 t. salt**

Stir in **5 cups of flour**, one at a time.

Knead with addition 1 cup, +/-, until you have a smooth elastic dough. Let dough rise 1 ½ to 2 hours. Divide and braid into two loaves. Place on a cookie sheet on which you have sprinkled 1/3 c. cornmeal.

Let rise one hour. Preheat oven to 350 degrees. Beat one egg and 1 T. water; brush over bread and sprinkle with poppy seeds. Bake 30 – 35 minutes. Cool completely before cutting.

To braid: Divide dough in half. Divide each half into three parts and roll each into a ball. Mist with vegetable cooking spray, cover and allow to rest for 20 minutes to relax the gluten. Working quickly to minimize handling the dough, roll each piece into a cigar shaped strand or log about eight inches long, a little plumper in the middle than at the ends. Lay the strands side by side. I prefer to begin in the middle, but you can begin at the end, as well. Cross the right hand strand over the center strand, then the left hand strand over the center, continuing until you reach the end. Tuck the tail of dough under and pinch to seal. Flip the loaf over, and also back to front, and braid the other half the same way.

8
Just Desserts

See's Fudge (or a close approximation)

In a large bowl: 1 c. chopped nuts

6 oz. Package of chocolate chips

1 cube melted margarine (or butter)

In a heavy saucepan: 2 c. sugar

1 small can evaporated milk

10 large marshmallows

Slowly bring to boil. Boil six minutes. Pour hot mixture over contents of bowl. Stir until chocolate is melted. Pour into greased dish and cool before cutting.

Pie Crust Mix (For those who bake pies often)

| 3# can Crisco | 16 cups flour | 8 tsp. Salt |

Combine as for pie crust, e.g. with two knives, your hands, or a pie crust blender. Your preference!

Store in air tight container on shelf, always ready for use. No messy measuring every time you want to make a pie. A little over two cups of this with 2 T. cold water added for each cup of mix makes a generous two-crust pie. Knead together until it holds a ball. Helps to chill a bit at this point, but not essential.

For Two-Crust Pie Dough Recipe

2 c. flour
2/3 c. Crisco
½ tsp. Salt
¼ c. ice cold water (plus or minus, depending on flour, humidity, etc.)

Roll out on generously floured cloth. Don't be afraid to handle this dough. Helps to chill for a few minutes after mixing.

Note: America's Test Kitchen recommends using vodka for part of the water for easy rolling out and flakier pie crust. For instance, instead of adding more water, add vodka.

Chess Pie

1 c. sugar
1 T. cream
½ c. chopped nuts
1 tsp. Vanilla

½ c. melted butter
2 eggs, slightly beaten
½ c. raisins

Pour the above mixture into unbaked pie crust. No top crust. Bake a few minutes at preheated 400 degree oven; reduce heat to 350 degrees and bake for 20 minutes or until set.

Rhubarb-Apple Pie

4 c. fruit (I like to combine rhubarb and sliced apples)
1 egg
3 T. flour
1 c. sugar

Round up in an unbaked pie shell. Cover with a lattice work crust or top with second crust. Wrap excess top crust under bottom crust edge, pressing edges together to seal. Flute using your two thumbs around edge of crust. Cut slits or shapes in several places in top crust. Bake at 450 degrees for 15 minutes. Reduce heat to 350 degrees for additional 45 minutes or until rhubarb is tender.

Lemon Meringue Pie

Prick bottom of an unbaked pie. Bake until lightly golden brown. Cool.

Filling: ½ c. sugar   ½ stick butter
         ½ c. fresh lemon juice   1 T. grated lemon rind

      2 large whole eggs and 1 egg yolk, lightly beaten

Combine first four ingredients in pan. Stir in beaten egg mixture. Cook over moderately high heat, stirring constantly until it coats the back of the spoon. Let cool for a few minutes. Pour into baked pie shell and cover with meringue (see below); be sure it comes to edges of crust.

Meringue:

   2 large egg whites
   Pinch cream of tartar
   ½ c. sugar

Beat eggs until stiff. Gradually add sugar.

Bake at 300 degrees for 30 minutes or until lightly browned.

Libby's Famous Pumpkin Pie

4 eggs, slightly beaten   2 tsp. Cinnamon
29 oz. Can pumpkin   1 tsp. Ginger 1
½ c. sugar   ½ tsp. Cloves
1 tsp. Salt   2 -12 oz. Cans evaporated milk

Combine filling ingredients in order given. Pour into two unbaked pie shells. Bake 15 minutes at 425 degrees; reduce heat to 350 and bake an additional 40-50 minutes or until knife inserted near center comes out clean. Cool.

Mincemeat Pie

Into an unbaked pie shell pour the contents of a jar of Borden's None Such Mincemeat. (This can be hard to find these days in supermarkets. I order it from www.amazon.com, both in boxed condensed version and jar that does not need to be reconstituted. Cover with second crust, tucking excess under; flute.

Mile High Ice Cream Pie

Into a cooled baked pie shell layer two of your favorite ice cream flavors, e.g. 1 pt. Vanilla ice cream and 1 pt. Chocolate. Return to freezer.

Beat until soft peaks form: 4 egg whites
½ tsp. Vanilla
¼ tsp. Cream of tartar

Gradually add ½ c. granulated sugar, beating until stiff and glossy and sugar is dissolved. Spread meringue over ice cream to edges of pastry. Broil 30 seconds to one minute to brown meringue. Freeze at least several hours. When pie is frozen wrap tightly if you plan to store for more than 24 hours. At serving time, drizzle chocolate sauce over each serving. Serves 8 – 12.

Just About the Best Hot Fudge You've Ever Eaten

3 oz. Bittersweet chocolate, chopped
1 1/3 sticks butter, cut into pieces

½ c. Droste (or other good quality cocoa, sifted and combined with
½ c. granulated sugar
½ c. brown sugar

2/3 c. heavy cream

Melt chocolate and butter over low heat. Add cocoa/sugar mixture. Add cream. Cook until it just reaches the boiling point. Makes about 2 cups and keeps a month if you can keep it locked up in the refrigerator!

Caramel Sauce/ Salted Caramel Sauce

1 cup brown sugar
¼ cup light corn syrup
1/3 cup whipping cream
3 Tbsp. butter
1 tsp. vanilla

For salted caramel, add ½ - 1 tsp. coarse sea salt. Add salt to desired saltiness.

Cook sugar, syrup and whip cream over medium heat for 5-6 minutes or until it reaches 230 degrees on candy thermometer. Stir in butter and vanilla and salt, if using. Serve warm. Refrigerate. When reheating, do not allow it to boil or it will get grainy and harden when put on ice cream.

Crème Brulée

4 ½ c. heavy cream (I use half and half and it's almost as good)
1 tsp. Vanilla extract
½ tsp. Salt
½ c. sugar
8 egg yolks

Preheat oven to 350 degrees. Whisk all ingredients together. Divide into oven safe ramekins. Place in deep baking dish. Fill baking dish with water to halfway up the sides of the ramekins. Cover with foil. Bake on middle rack of oven for 30 – 40 minutes, until custard sets. Carefully remove from oven and cool completely on a rack. When ready to serve sprinkle each with granulated sugar and burn carefully with small propane torch.

One Point Crème Brulée (Weight Watcher's Style)

1 1/3 c. non-fat milk
1 T. + 1 tsp. Non-fat dry milk
½ c. Egg Beaters
¼ c. Splenda
1 Tbsp. + 1 tsp. Sugar
1 tsp. Vanilla

Stir together ½ cup milk and non-fat dry milk until blended. Stir in remaining non-fat milk., Egg Beaters, 1/4 c. Splenda and vanilla. Pour mixture in ramekins or custard cups. Bake in pan filled with hot water to 1 inch depth in 325 degree oven for 35 minutes or until custard is set. Continue = sprinkle sugar and burn carefully! Note: *Bear in mind, this is not the super-rich, thick (15 point) crème brulée that you will get with the recipe above or in a fine restaurant, but for 14 points less those interested in their waistline will appreciate its goodness – it's still rich and creamy.*

Blackberry Cobbler – My favorite

1 stick Butter
1-1/4 cup Sugar
1 cup Self-Rising Flour
1 cup Milk
2 cups Blackberries (frozen Or Fresh)

Melt butter in a microwavable dish. Pour 1 cup of sugar and flour into a mixing bowl, whisking in milk. Mix well. Then, pour in melted butter and whisk it all well together. Butter a baking dish.

Now rinse and pat dry the blackberries. Pour the batter into the buttered baking dish. Sprinkle blackberries over the top of the batter; distributing evenly. Sprinkle ¼ cup sugar over the top.

Bake in the oven at 350 degrees for 1 hour, or until golden and bubbly. If you desire, sprinkle an additional teaspoon of sugar over the cobbler 10 minutes before it's done.

Raspberry/Blackberry/Apple/Peach – Any Fruit Cobbler

½ to ¾ c. sugar   ¾ tsp. cinnamon

1 T. cornstarch   ½ c. water

6 ½ c. fruit, cut up if necessary

1. Mix well and place in baking dish. Preheat oven to 400 degrees.
2. Mix the following until creamy:
   - ¼ c. sugar
   - ¼ c. butter
   - ½ c. milk
3. Add and mix well:
   - ¼ tsp. Baking soda
   - 1 tsp. Baking powder
   - 1 cup all-purpose flour
4. Drop batter in eight equal spoonsful over fruit. Bake 35 – 40 minutes.

Note: I like combinations of fruit in this – rhubarb and apples; peaches or nectarines with apples; raspberries, blackberries and apples; or just plain apples are delicious, too. Adjust sweetness to tartness of fruit. Top with ice cream or whipped topping.

Bananas Foster

1 T. butter
2 T. brown sugar
1 ripe banana, peeled and halved lengthwise
Dash of cinnamon
1 oz. White rum

Melt butter in fry pan or chafing dish. Add brown sugar and blend well.
Add banana and sauté. Sprinkle with cinnamon. Pour over liqueur and
ignite, basting banana with flaming liquid. Serve over vanilla ice cream
when flame dies out. Serves 1.

New Orleans Style Bread Pudding

Heat oven to 350 degrees and prepare a 9 x 13 inch baking dish by buttering
well.
Combine:

    1 quart milk
    3 egg yolks
    ¼ c. granulated sugar
    ½ tsp. Salt
    ¼ tsp. Nutmeg

Add: 1 T. vanilla
       2-4 T. melted butter
½ to 1 cup raisins
Pour over 2 cups cubed bread.
Beat the whites of the three eggs until stiff.
Gently fold into pudding mixture. Pour into greased pan. Bake until set and
lightly browned on top. Serve warm with a bit of hard sauce on top. (I zap it
in the microwave to heat slightly, if necessary.)

Hard Sauce: 1/3 c. butter, 1 cup powdered sugar, 1 tsp. Vanilla or
brandy/rum if desired.

Pavlova *(Learned from Kate Morice, our New Zealand friend '72)*

3 large or 4 small egg whites
1 ¼ c. sugar   pinch of salt
3 T. cold water   ½ tsp. Vanilla
1 T. vinegar   3 tsp. Cornstarch

Beat egg whites until they begin to peak. Gradually add sugar and water alternatively 1 T. at a time. You beat this beyond the time you think. Then salt, vinegar and vanilla. Then gently fold in cornstarch. Spread on greased foil on a pan. Bake 275 degrees for one hour. Turn off the oven and leave in for another hour.

Garnish with whipped cream and strawberries and/or kiwi. (My secret tip about whipping cream: add a teaspoon of KNOX gelatin dissolved in a teaspoon or so of hot water as you are whipping and adding the sugar will keep it from separating and getting watery. Trust me!)

Quick, Easy and Impressive – Thompson Seedless Grapes

Mix together: sour cream and brown sugar to sweeten

Pour over separated Thompson seedless grapes. Marinate in refrigerator until ready to serve in a pretty glass!

Another Quick and Easy – Ambrosia

Can of crushed pineapple, well drained
Can of mandarin oranges
Seedless Grapes, optional
Some people add shredded coconut, too.

Stir in enough whipped topping to hold together.
Chill…and serve in a pretty bowl.

Another Unusual, easy one – Avocado Delight!

2 large avocados   ¾ c. sugar
¼ c. whipped cream, whipped or whipped topping
¼ c. lemon juice   ¼ tsp. Salt

Blend avocados in Cuisinart with lemon juice. Mix all together. Chill and serve with a bit of whipped cream on top.

French Strawberry Pie

1 pie shell, baked   1 large package cream cheese
1 quart fresh strawberries   1 c. sugar
3 T. cornstarch

Spread cream cheese that has been blended with a small amount of cream or milk into previously baked and cooled pie shell. Wash and stem the berries. Arrange one half of berries with hulled side down. Mash remaining berries. Bring to boil. Slowly add sugar and cornstarch that have been mixed together. Simmer for about ten minutes, stirring as it thickens. Spread over uncooked berries in pie shell. Chill. Serve with whipped cream.

Carrot Cake (heavy and nutty)

1 1/3 c. sugar   1 c. raisins
1 ½ c. water   1 c. grated
   carrots
2 T. butter   ½
   tsp. Cloves 1 T. cinnamon
    1 T. nutmeg

Pour all of the above in a saucepan. Boil slowly for 5 – 7 minutes. Cool.

Add: 1 c. walnuts
            2 c. flour (or 1 c. flour, 1 cup Krusteaz Pancake mix.
          Pinch salt   2 tsp. Soda   2 eggs

Bake at 350 degrees.

Honey Spice Cake

¾ c. whole wheat flour 1 tsp. Cinnamon
½ tsp. Baking soda ½ tsp. Nutmeg
¼ tsp. Cloves ¼ tsp. Allspice

Combine, mixing well. Add the following ingredients and beat well:

1 Tbsp. Applesauce ½ c. plain non-fat yogurt
1 egg or ¼ c. Egg Beaters 2 T. honey
1 T. brown sugar 1 tsp. Vanilla
¾ c. raisins

Pour into small loaf pan. Bake about 25 minutes or until it pulls away from pan, indicating it is done. Let cool 10 minutes. Then turn out onto rack to cool.

Gingerbread (This is a great one!)

Combine and bring to a boil:

½ c. molasses and ½ # butter

Let cool a bit while you cream: 1 egg
                                    1 cup sugar

Add: 2 ¼ c. flour
       1 ½ tsp. Soda
       1 ½ tsp. Ginger
       1 tsp. Cinnamon
       ½ tsp. Cloves
       ¼ tsp. Nutmeg
       Grated peel of one orange
       ¼ tsp. Salt

Add molasses mixture and ½ c. boiling water. Then add ½ c. sour cream. Mix thoroughly. Bake 50 minutes in a 9 x 13 inch pan at 350 degrees. Top with whipping cream or applesauce.

Mississippi Mud Cake

Preheat oven to 275 degrees.   1 ½ hour baking time

Sift together: 2 c. flour   1 tsp. Baking soda
                    Pinch salt

Heat five minutes in top of double boiler: 1 ¾ c. coffee
                                              ¼ c. bourbon

Add: 5 oz. Unsweetened chocolate
          2 sticks of butter, cut into pieces.

Heat mixture, stirring until chocolate and butter are melted. Remove from heat.

Stir in: 2 cups sugar

Let cool three minutes and then transfer to bowl. Add flour mixture one half cup at a time, beating at medium speed. Continue beating for one minute.

Add: 2 eggs, lightly beaten
          1 tsp. Vanilla

Beat until batter is smooth. Pour batter into 9" tube pan, which has been greased and dusted with cocoa. Bake for 1 ½ hour at 300 degrees. Cool completely in pan on rack. Remove from pan. Serve with whipped cream, sweetened and flavored with white crème de cocoa to taste.

Pumpkin Cake Roll

Beat 3 eggs on high speed for five minutes (very important step!) Gradually add 1 cup granulated sugar. Stir in 2/3 c. pumpkin and 1 tsp. Lemon juice.

In separate bowl, stir together: ¾ c. flour ½ tsp. Nutmeg
1 tsp. baking powder   ½ tsp. Salt
1 tsp. Ginger

Fold into pumpkin mixture and spread in greased and floured 15x1 jelly roll pan or sided cookie sheet. Top with 1 cup finely chopped walnuts. Bake at 375 degrees for 15 minutes. Turn out onto towel that has been sprinkled with powdered sugar. Starting at narrow end, roll towel and cake together. Let cool.

Filling: Cream well: 6 oz. Cream cheese 4 T. butter
1 c. powdered sugar ½ tsp. Vanilla
(I like some orange rind, too. Optional)

Roll cake out and frost. Roll again (but without the towel now, of course, just using the towel to help you roll it. Refrigerate. Makes about 8 servings.

The Cake Mix Doctor Cookbook **by Anne Byrn** has a great collection of ways to adapt cake mixes to personalize them and make them even more delicious than those you can purchase at a bakery. I especially like their Carrot Cake with Cream Cheese frosting.

Carrot Cake from the Cake Mix Doctor

1 package plain yellow cake mix
1 package vanilla instant pudding
2/3 c. fresh orange juice
½ c. vegetable oil
4 large eggs
2 teaspoons ground cinnamon
3 cups grated carrots
½ c. raisins
½ cup chopped walnuts or pecans
Fresh Orange Cream Cheese Frosting

Generously grease two 9-inch cake pans; dust with flour and shake out excess. Preheat oven to 350 degrees. (Serves 16)

Place the cake mix, pudding mix, orange juice, oil, eggs and cinnamon in large bowl. Blend with mixer on low speed for one minute. Scrape down sides of bowl. Increase speed to medium and beat 2 minutes more. Gently fold in carrots, raisins and nuts. Divide the batter between the prepared pans.

Bake until they are golden brown and spring back when lightly pressed with your finger – 30 – 35 minutes. Remove the pans from oven and place on wire rack to cool for 10 minutes. Run a dinner knife around edge of each layer and invert onto rack, then invert each again onto another rack so that the cakes are right side up. Allow to cool completely.

Meanwhile prepare the icing:

Fresh Orange Cream Cheese Frosting

1 package cream cheese (8 oz.)
8 Tbsp. Butter, at room temperature 3
cups confectioner's sugar, sifted
2 Tbsp. Fresh orange juice
1 Tbsp. Grated orange zest

Blend the cream cheese and butter in large bowl with electric mixer.
Add the confectioner's sugar, a bit at a time, blending on low speed
until the sugar is well combined. Then add the orange juice and zest.
Continue beating until frosting lightens and is fluffy. (Be prepared to
add a bit more confectioner's sugar if it appears too runny, but it will
harden some in the refrigerator after you've iced the cake.

After icing tops and sides of each layer, place the cake, uncovered, in
the refrigerator until the frosting sets – 20 minutes or so. You may
cover the cake and store in refrigerator for up to one week (if your will
power is really STRONG!).

Layer Cake Like Mom Used to Make

1 package plain white cake mix
1 cup whole milk
8 T. butter, melted
3 large eggs
 2 tsp. Vanilla extract
One recipe of Fluffy Chocolate Frosting

Fluffy Chocolate Frosting

1 cube butter (room temperature)
2/3 c. Fluffy Chocolate Frosting good quality cocoa
3 c. confectioner's sugar, sifted if needed
1/3 c. whole milk (room temperature)
2 tsp. Vanilla ¼
tsp. Salt

Mix until smooth and fluffy. Enough for a two or three layer cake.

The Loopy Ewe Pumpkin Dessert

1   large can pumpkin (28 - 30 oz.)
1   can evaporated milk (10 - 12 oz.)
3   eggs
2   sticks butter or margarine
1   cup sugar
1   tsp. Cinnamon, nutmeg, cloves, allspice or pumpkin pie spice -- (I probably used a bit more than a teaspoon)
1   box yellow cake mix
1   cup nuts (optional)
2

In a large bowl, combine the pumpkin, evaporated milk, eggs, sugar and cinnamon.

Line a 9 x 13 pan with foil and grease it. (I just greased liberally and sprayed with Pam.) Pour the pumpkin mixture in the pan and sprinkle the dry cake mix on top. Pat the cake mix down with a spoon. Sprinkle with nuts (if desired) and drizzle the melted butter over the top. Bake at 350 degrees for 1 hour (check it at 45 minutes and put a piece of foil over the top if it's getting a little brown.) Let stand 10 minutes and turn out on a board to cut into pieces, or refrigerate. Great served with whipped topping or ice cream.

NOTES: Quick and easy...I made this and took it to Laurie's for Sunday after Thanksgiving dinner.

Cookies

My Favorite Oatmeal Cookies – Prize Winner!!!

1 cup shortening   1 c. granulated sugar
1 c. brown sugar   2 large eggs 2 tsp.
Vanilla   3 c. oatmeal
1 ½ c. flour   1 tsp. Salt
1 tsp. Cinnamon   1 tsp. soda
1 ½ c. coconut
1 c. coarsely chopped macadamia nuts or walnuts

Cream shortening with sugars, eggs and vanilla. Add dry ingredients, coconut, and nuts. Bake at 350 degrees for 8 – 10 minutes or until lightly browned. Cool 2 – 3 minutes before removing from baking sheet. They firm up as they cool.

Poor Man Cookies

Bring to boil: 1 cup raisins in 2 cups water
Simmer until approximately 1 cup liquid remains. Cool slightly and add:
   ½ c. margarine or butter   1 c. sugar
   1 tsp. Soda   1 egg
   1 tsp. Allspice   2 c. flour
   1 tsp. cinnamon   1 tsp. cloves

(If you use only 1 cup flour, it makes a nice pudding like dessert; top with whipped topping.)

Mix and pour into greased jelly roll pan. Bake at 350 degrees for 20 – 2 minutes. Glaze with thin powdered sugar frosting. (I like the glaze made with lemon or orange juice.)

Cookie Jar Gingersnaps

Cream together: ¾ c. shortening

1 cup sugar

1 egg

¼ cup. Molasses

Stir in: 2 c. flour   1 T. ginger
2 tsp. Baking soda   1 tsp. Cinnamon   ½
   tsp. Salt

Form into small balls and roll in granulated sugar. (I use meatball scoop!)
Allow room on pan for them to spread out during baking. Place on greased
cookie sheet. Bake at 350 degrees for 10-12 minutes. Makes 4 dozen.

For holiday cookies, you can dip cooled cookies in 1 ½ cups white chocolate
chips melted with 1 ½ T. Crisco. Dip cookie half way and then lay on waxed
paper until set. Add colored sprinkles if you like.

Nutballs

Mix together:
      ½# butter
      4 tsp. Gran. Sugar
       Vanilla
      2 c. sifted flour
      2 cups chopped walnuts

Form in small balls and place on ungreased cookie sheet. Bake 30 minutes at
320 degrees. Roll in powdered sugar while still hot.

Oatmeal Crisps

1 c. shortening	1 tsp. Salt
1 c. brown sugar	1 tsp. Soda
1 c. granulated sugar	2 cup quick cooking oats
2 eggs	½ cup. chopped nuts
1 tsp. Vanilla	chocolate chips (optional)
1 ½ c. flour	

Cream shortening and sugars. Add eggs and vanilla. Beat. Add flour, salt, soda, oatmeal, nuts, etc. Bake 350 degrees for 10 minutes. Makes 5 doz.

Almond Roca Bars (Perhaps my favorite!)

Cream together:

1 c. butter
½ c. brown sugar
½ c. sugar
1 T. vanilla
1 egg yolk
2 c. sifted flour

Spread in jelly roll pan or cookie sheet with sides. Bake 15 minutes at 350 degrees. Meanwhile melt one package German Sweet Chocolate. Spread on still warm pastry. Sprinkle immediately with 1 cup finely chopped nuts. (Pat in a bit so that they don't fall off.) Cut while still warm.

Caramel Chocolate Bars

(These are sinfully delicious – get help with unwrapping the caramels. That's the toughest part of this recipe!)

1 14 oz. Package of Kraft caramels
¾ c. Eagle brand condensed milk
1 package of German Sweet Chocolate Cake mix
1/3 c. evaporated milk
¾ c. melted butter
1 cup nuts
6 oz. Package chocolate chips

Melt caramels in condensed milk in top of double boiler. In a large bowl, add 1 package of cake mix, evaporated milk, melted butter and chopped nuts.

Butter bottom and sides of 9 x 13 inch baking dish. Spread one-half of cake mix batter on bottom and bake for 6 minutes at 350 degrees. Spread chocolate chips over it and then caramel mix. Spread rest of cake mix. Bake for 15 to 18 minutes longer.

Date Nut Pinwheels

Mix together: ½ c. shortening
                 1 cup brown sugar
                 1 egg

Stir in: 1 T. cream (or sour cream)
                 1 tsp. Vanilla

Sift together and stir in:
                 1 ¾ c. flour
                 ½ tsp. Soda
                 ½ tsp. Cream of tartar
                 1/8 tsp. Salt

Mix together until smooth. Divide into two parts. Roll into rectangle 11 x 7. Spread each with date nut mixture below. Roll up tightly. Chill. Cut into ¼ inch slices. Bake about 10 minutes in 400 degree oven.

Filling: Cook until smooth and paste-like the following:

   1 cup chopped dates
   ½ c. water
   Lemon juice
   Vanilla
   ½ c. finely chopped walnuts

Cherry Bars

Part I:

    ½ c. butter   2 T. powdered sugar 1 c. flour

Cut butter into flour and powdered sugar, as in making pie dough. Spread in 9 x 13 inch baking dish and bake for 20 minutes at 350 degrees. Cool and spread with the following:

Mix: 2 eggs
     1 c. sugar
     1/4 c. flour
     1/2 tsp. Baking powder
     1/8 tsp. Salt
     1 tsp. Vanilla
     3 oz. Bottle of maraschino cherries, finely chopped, with juice.
     3/4 c. walnuts, finely chopped

Bake for 15 minutes longer or until lightly browned on top. Cool slightly. Cut into squares while still warm.

Lemon Bars (Per Florence Callaway)

Cream **1/2 cup softened butter** with **1/4 cup powdered sugar**.
Add **1 c. flour** and **1/4 tsp. Salt**. Beat until mixed.
Pour mixture into greased 8 x 8 inch pan, spreading by hand. Bake at 350
degrees for 15 minutes.

Meanwhile, combine **2 slightly beaten eggs**.
Add **1 c. sugar**.
Add grated rind from one lemon.
Add **2 T. flour** and **2 T. lemon juice**. Mix well.

After crust has baked for 15 minutes, open oven and pour the liquid on top of the
crust. Bake 20 minutes longer at 350 degrees. Sift on light coating of powdered
sugar while still warm.

Heather's Secret, Secret Chocolate Chip Oatmeal Cookies

½ c. oil	½ tsp. Salt
½ c. margarine	½ tsp. Baking powder
1 c. sugar	1 tsp. Soda
2 eggs	2 c. flour
1 c. brown sugar	2 c. oatmeal
6 oz. Chocolate chips	½ c. peanuts or walnuts
½ - 1 cup raisins	

Add all ingredients in large mixing bowl. Mix until smooth. Bake at 350
degrees on ungreased cookie sheet for 8 – 10 minutes.

Black Bean Brownies

1 can of black beans, rinsed and drained
3 Tbsp. applesauce (or oil)
3 large eggs
¾ cup sugar (Splenda)
¼ cup Hershey's cocoa powder
Pinch salt
1 tsp. instant coffee mix or Espresso powder
¼ cup chocolate chips

Mix all ingredients except chocolate chips in blender until smooth. Pour into lined 8 x 8" baking pan. Sprinkle chocolate chips and chopped walnuts over all. Bake at 350 degrees for approximately 30 minutes – until begins to pull away from sides of pan and top is dry.

9

HOLIDAY RECIPES

Back in the day…no Christmas cookie tray or gift box was ever complete without the following (in cookie section above):

    Almond Roca Bars
    Cherry Bars
    Lemon Bars
    Date Nut Pinwheels

In more recent times, we have been making Nancy Henry's English Toffee and Creamy Caramels.

Egg Nog

1 dozen eggs, separated

Beat ½ pound powdered sugar into well-beaten egg yolks (should be almost lemon-colored). Add 2 cups bourbon. Let set for an hour or so. Add 1 can evaporated milk and (2 more cups of bourbon – optional) Add 2 oz. vanilla and 2 quarts of whole milk. Refrigerate and let stand overnight, if possible.

Beat egg whites until stiff. Fold in just before serving. Sprinkle with freshly grated nutmeg.

Mulled Wine

1 gallon apple juice

In a cheesecloth bag place:
    80 whole cloves
    6 cinnamon sticks
    Rind of 4 lemons and 2 oranges

Simmer for ½ hour. Remove spices and add juice of 4 lemons. Add 1 gallon burgundy and (1 quart port – optional). Head through.

Champagne Punch

1 bottles champagne
1 to 2 quarts soca
½ fifth brandy
¼ bottle Sweet and Sour Mix
1/3 bottle Curacaou

Ice and orange slices

The House That Gingerbread Built

We've all been intimidated by the photos. Page after colorful page of the most amazing gingerbread houses you've ever seen - gables and verandahs, Santa's workshop or Buckingham Palace. And you say "Forget it." Too bad, because it's not that hard and it's a lot of fun. This recipe proves it, as long as you remember the following points: (1) it will take all weekend (2) don't panic (3) have everything ready before you start. Great fun for the children to decorate...and EAT!

Things you will need: a board or something stiff on which to place the house; candies, a parchment or cloth cone from which to pipe icing.

The Gingerbread Recipe

1 cup shortening
5 cups flour
1 cup dark brown sugar
1 cup dark molasses
2 eggs
2 Tbsp. Vinegar
1   tsp. Allspice
3   tsp. Cloves
4   tsp. Cinnamon
3 tsp. Ginger
1   ½ tsp. Nutmeg
2   tsp. Baking powder
1   tsp. Baking soda

Mix dry ingredients and set aside. Mix other ingredients and add to dry. Form dough into two separate balls. Wrap in Saran and chill for two to three hours. Roll out on back of cookie sheet and cut out shapes, leaving space between. Remove scraps and keep rolling until all shapes are formed. You will need two rectangles that are 4 x 5 (sides); two that are 6 ½ x 7 (roof); and two end panels that are peaked to form the roof (4 x 6 to a peak in the center of the 6"sie that goes to 8"). Bake dough at 325 degrees for 10 to 20 minutes and then turn heat down to dry out a few minutes longer, but not brown around edges.

Caramel Syrup Glue for assembling gingerbread houses):

1 cup granulated sugar
½ cup light corn syrup
½ c. water

Mix ingredients in heavy saucepan. Bring to a boil over a medium flame; stir occasionally. Cook without stirring, until the liquid is golden brown. Remove from heat and cool until bubbles subside.

Assembly: It helps to have an extra pair of hands during this phase. Draw a rectangle on the base to position the house. Dry fit all the pieces to make sure everything lines up. Even out all the surfaces that will be joined to another surface with 50 grade sandpaper.

With a metal spatula, spread hot syrup along the bottom of the back wall and place it on base. Do the same with the front wall. With someone holding the front and back wall, spread two wide strips of syrup on the underside of one of the roof pieces, and place atop the walls. Repeat this for the other roof piece. With royal icing in a piping bag, reinforce the outside of all joints.

Royal Icing

Fluff **six egg whites** with mixer. Gradually add **4 tsp. Cream of tartar** and **two pounds of powdered sugar** a half cup at a time, and beat at high speed for 7 to 10- minutes until a knife drawn through it leaves a clear path which holds its shape.

Decorate: This is the fun part. Use hard candies, chocolate chips, marshmallows, M & M's, gumdrops, licorice. Use your imagination!

The Gingerbread Book by Allen D. Bragdon has fabulous designs for the holidays and more. I made monster cookies for one of Max's birthday parties with the following recipe. The kids had great fun painting the cookies I had already prepared for them.

Basic Honey Gingerbread Dough

7 ½ c. unsifted flour
4 tsp. Ground cinnamon
1   T. ground ginger
1   T. baking soda
1 ½ tsp. Nutmeg
½ tsp. Salt
1 ½ cups butter or margarine
1 ½ cups firmly packed dark brown sugar
¾ c. honey
3 eggs

Combine dry ingredients. Cream butter, sugar and honey. Add dry ingredients a cup at a time. Cover bowl and refrigerate several hours before rolling out and cutting cookies. Roll dough out on foil lined cookie sheet, cutting around cookie pattern, ¼-inch thickness. Remove excess and chill for later use. Bake in 350 degree oven for 12-15 minutes or until cookies are firm and lightly browned. Cool completely before removing cookies from foil.

Decorating: Use royal icing in a piping bag to make outlines. Flow frosting made with diluted royal icing can be colored and brushed on or applied with cone and spread with toothpick. If you are using two colors in one area, work with only one color at a time, allowing it to dry at least an hour before applying another, so that the two will not bleed together.

Fun Pre-Thanksgiving Project with Children – Placecards (From www.ourbestbites.com)

Ingredients/Supplies

Oreo Cookies
Candy Corn
Whoppers
Peanut butter Cups
Chocolate frosting
Yellow Frosting   (You can use those prefilled tubes from the baking aisle.)
Optional: Red frosting
Optional: black sprinkles for eyes

First step: Grab a cookie Add a little more chocolate frosting. Stick in tips of candy corn.

Next put a dab of frosting on the opposite end of the cookie and secure it to the "base" cookie. It helps to place them next to a wall as they dry so they stay put.

While those are drying, unwrap your PB cups. Take a sharp knife and cut a sliver off of one end

Place a dab of frosting on the peanut butter cup, and place it on the cookie like so. Next glue a Whopper on with frosting in front of peanut butter cup.

While they are lying there, use a dab of frosting (I use yellow) and glue on the white tip of a candy corn for a beak. Put two yellow dots on for eyes, and for the black spots in the eyes you can use a dab of yellow frosting and a sprinkle.

Once the beak stays put you can flip them over and draw on some little yellow feet. If you have red frosting too (usually comes in a set with the tube of yellow) you can add a little gobble gobble wattle.

Candy from Nancy Henry's Files:

DIVINITY FUDGE

2 cups sugar
½ cup corn syrup
½ cup water
1 teaspoon vanilla extract
½ cup chopped nuts
1/8 teaspoon salt
2 egg whites – stiffly beaten

1. Boil sugar, water and corn syrup to 250° F (or to a hard ball stage). This ball will make a crackling sound when tapped against the side of cup.
2. Pour syrup into stiffly beaten egg whites, beating constantly.
3. When dull and stiff enough to hold its shape add vanilla, nuts & salt.
4. Drop by spoonsful onto waxed paper or press into a buttered pan and cut into squares.

CREAMY CARAMELS (I make these every year with a little help from my friend – everyone appreciates receiving them. .Great gift!)

    2 cups granulated white sugar
    Dash salt
    2 cups light corn syrup
    1/2 cup butter
    2 cups half and half
    1 teaspoon vanilla

1. Put sugar and corn syrup + salt into large heavy saucepan; heat to boiling, boil to firm ball stage, 255◻ F, stirring occasionally.
2. Gradually add butter and milk so slowly that mixture does not stop boiling at any time.
3. Continue to cook rapidly with constant stirring to medium ball stage (242 ◻ F) – about 30-40 minutes. The candy will stick and scorch easily toward the last, so be careful to stir constantly.
4. Remove from heat, add flavoring and stir well; then pour into buttered 9 – inch square baking dish/pan. [I line pan with foil to make for easier removal for cutting.]
5. Cool thoroughly before cutting. When cool, turn out onto cutting board. Cut into small squares with sharp, heavy knife using a sawing motion. Wrap in 4x4 squares of waxed paper, twisting ends. Makes 2 pounds.

VARIATIONS: **Chocolate caramels:** (UNTRIED BECAUSE THE BASIC CANDY IS SO GOOD!)

Melt 3 squares unsweetened chocolate over hot water in the pan in which the candy is to be cooked; to this add the sugar, salt & corn syrup; proceed as above.

NUTS: Just before pouring add ½ cup coarsely chopped pecans or walnuts.

English Toffee (Almond Roca-like)

1/2 #   margarine
1/4 pound butter
1 1/2 cups sugar
4 ounces almonds or walnuts -- (or walnuts),
chopped
8 ounces chocolate bar or chocolate chips (If you
plan to frost both sides, double this.)
 1/2 cup almonds or walnuts -- chopped finely (or more if you want to throw
some on the cookie sheet before pouring on the toffee.)

Turn electric fry pan (or burner) to high and melt butter and margarine; add sugar
stirring constantly.

After five minutes, add about 4 ounces of almonds and then cook as before for
about five minutes. Do not let mixture get too brown, as light mahogany is
desired color. About 290-300 degrees on candy thermometer. (Brittle ball
stage when a half teaspoonful is dropped into cold water.)

Pour into ungreased cookie sheet or Silpat pad, pouring off excess butter.
Smooth to desired thickness. (I use a Silpat pad in bottom of cookie sheet as
that makes it very easy to remove.) Cool.

Meanwhile, melt chocolate in double boiler, one half at a time. When candy is
cool, frost top half and sprinkle with nuts. If desired, you can turn over and
repeat melting chocolate, etc. When thoroughly cool - about three hours, break
into small pieces and serve or place in tin for storage.

Note: I have a severe weak spot for this candy during the holiday season. I can
resist fruitcake, all manner of Christmas cookies, puddings and mince pies. But
when it comes to almond Roca, will power abandons me.

Five-Minute Fudge Wreath (Great gift item)

12 oz. bag semisweet chocolate morsels
9   ounces butterscotch morsels (about ¾ of a bag.)
1 can sweetened condensed milk
1 teaspoon vanilla extract
8 oz. walnut halves
1/2   cup currants
Candied cherries, red and green, for garnish, optional

Prepare an 8" cake pan with butter. (I use one that has removable bottom.) Cover the empty condensed milk can with plastic food wrap and center it in the cake pan.

Place a heavy pot on the stove and preheat it over low heat. Add chips and milk and stir until chips are melted and milk combined. Note: Save the empty condensed milk can. Stir in vanilla and remove fudge from heat. Add nuts and currants and stir in immediately.

Spoon fudge into pan around can, making sure to re-center can if it drifts.

The fudge will set up almost immediately. Garnish can only be added in the first minute or two the fudge is in the pan, so work quickly. Decorate your wreath with "holly" made from cut candied red and green cherries. A wreath left plain can be garnished with a pretty fabric bow when serving. Chill covered in the refrigerator and slice fudge very thin when ready to serve, a little goes a long way.

Description:

"Plan to chill for a couple of hours before serving."

Yield: "2 pounds"   Start to Finish: 5 minutes

Variations of 5 minute wreath:

White Chocolate & Pistachio:

>White chocolate chips – 1 1 ½ oz. bag, plus 1 cup (no butterscotch!)
>Substitute 1 to 1 1/2 cups of shelled natural pistachio nuts for walnuts.
>Substitute 1/2 cup dried sweetened cranberries for currants.

Goober and Raisinette Wreath:

Original recipe, but:
>Swap peanut butter chips for butterscotch chips.
>Swap large whole peanuts for walnuts used in original recipe (such as peeled Virginia Peanuts)
>Swap 1/2 cup large raisins in place of currants in original recipe

SURVIVING THE MAKING AND PLANNING OF A
THANKSGIVING/CHRISTMAS DINNER

YES, the "Holidays" are here; the first big event is Thanksgiving. I was recently surfing the Food TV Network (my very favorite) and look what I found. A step-by-step game plan to help you go from frozen supermarket bird to beautifully set table without driving yourself crazy!

Mind you, this is not how I've ever done it. About the best I have done is order the fresh turkey ahead from Branigan's Turkey Farm (on occasion) or the prime rib for Christmas from Cracchiola's Market in Woodland – all ready to pop in the oven, deliciously seasoned. These, however, are the easiest meals for me...no debate about what to have. Tradition!

But this is how the hostess with the moistest would probably do it. Just sayin'...

Three weeks ahead:
- Prepare your guest list. Firm up how many people will be there. ☐ Find out if there are any special dietary needs for your guests.

Two weeks ahead:
- Decide on your final menu.
- Assign cooking projects to family members who offer to help. Tell volunteers how many people their dishes should serve.
- Order your fresh turkey or buy your frozen turkey and put it in the freezer.
- Shop for non-perishable goods now, before the rush. Make the Costco run. You can buy beverages, flour, sugar, brown sugar, corn syrup, canned pumpkin, fresh or frozen cranberries, etc. . . .

One week ahead:
- Shop for non-perishable vegetables, such as butternut squash, potatoes, carrots, parsnips and turnips.

- Buy heavy cream now. In the days before Thanksgiving, it can sometimes be hard to find.
- If necessary, wash and iron linens, polish silver, etc. Dig out your turkey roaster and platter and any serving dishes on high shelves. Don't wait until the morning of Thanksgiving to do that. **Three days ahead:**
  - Defrost! If you have a frozen turkey, clear a space in your fridge and put the bird in now so it will be fully defrosted on cooking day.
  - Organize the house. If you're having a lot of guests, you may want to set up the table and ensure you have enough chairs.

Two days ahead:

- Oh, they say bake as much as you can today. Make pumpkin pies or pumpkin cheesecake, as well as rolls, and breads, including cornbread for stuffing. Personally, two days seems a bit far ahead! Maybe delegate the pie baking?
- Make things that can sit for two days in the fridge such as soups, cranberry sauce, and items such as sweet potato balls or green bean casserole, which can be stored uncooked in the refrigerator to be baked on the day.

MAKE AHEAD GRAVY

You can't serve roast turkey without gravy. For several years Peter has called upon me to make gravy at the last minute. I'm no longer able to stand up long enough to make it – especially in someone else's kitchen. And even if I were, I would never make it day-of again.

When you are buying your turkey three or four days ahead, buy some extra wings. Preheat your oven to 375 degrees F. For 2 ½ cups of gravy, throw a couple of turkey wings in a roasting pan along with the following:

    4 ribs of celery, roughly chopped, leafs and all.

    1 onion, cut into chunks.

    4 cloves of garlic (optional)

Roast for a couple of hours. Remove from the oven and add 6 cups of water. Bring to a boil on top of the stove. Turn down heat and simmer on low for an hour or so, uncovered. The stock will reduce. Strain the stock. Throw away all the aromatics and turkey bones. They are all used up! Refrigerate liquid overnight. Remove the fat that has accumulated on top.

When you are ready to make gravy: Melt 4 Tbsp. butter.

At this point, I whisk flour into liquid, but you can also make a roux by whisking the flour directly into the butter and cook it for a few minutes to get rid of the flour taste. Whisk in 2 cups defatted turkey stock and cook until thickened. Add some milk – ½ cup whole milk, a teaspoon of cider vinegar and some Kosher salt. Gravy thickens as it sets, so you may want to add more liquid just before serving. If it's too thin, just make a flour and butter paste and add as you whisk.

MAKE AHEAD MASHED POTATOES

The perfect ratio for every 4 servings:
1 pound of Russet potatoes
½ cup of half and half
4 Tbsp. unsalted butter, melted

Peel, cut and rinse. Rinse them from getting too starchy. Cut them into similarly sized chunks.

Start the potatoes in cold, generously salted water. When cooked, while the potatoes are hot, add the melted butter, mashing to incorporate, coating the potatoes with the butter , then add hot liquid. This helps them from becoming gluey. Always add hot liquid to the potatoes. Store in covered dish in refrigerator.

30 minutes or so before you want to serve, preheat oven to 350 F. Cover baking dish with foil. Place the mashed potato-filled dish into a larger baking dish with high sides and place in the oven. Pour boiling water so that it comes halfway up the sides of the smaller dish. Heat for 20-30 minutes, depending on the size of pan, stirring half-way through. If you are short on oven space, the same method works on stove top by keeping the water on low simmer, stirring frequently until warmed through. Add a splash of milk to help thin out, if needed. To hold for an hour or two, just turn off the heat and cover the pot..

One day ahead:

- Set the table. It's easiest to do it now.
- Do any remaining baking, including that apple pie.
- Buy your salad greens and perishable vegetables. Wash lettuce leaves now, dry well, and store by packing them in paper towels in a plastic bag in the refrigerator.
- If you ordered a fresh turkey, pick it up from the turkey farm or butcher. (Or pick up prime rib.)
- Roast some turkey wings to make gravy drippings. Make gravy ahead and then just heat it up on day of.
- Calculate your cooking time for tomorrow and the sequence for your cooking. Figure out what time that turkey or prime rib needs to go in.
- Figure out what can't be cooked along with the turkey in the oven, either in terms of temperature or space. Plan to prepare those things before or after the turkey/prime rib is done, or on the stovetop while it's cooking – or better, make them earlier today.
- Be sure chairs are in place for the number of guests expected.
- Prepare your vegetables for cooking – cleaning, peeling, dicing. Cover the ready-to-go vegetables and put them in the refrigerator.

Thanksgiving Day:

First:
- Prepare stuffing for the turkey, plus extra to cook on the side.
- Stuff the turkey and get it (or the prime rib) in the oven according to the schedule you have already calculated.
- Add vegetables to roast for prime rib dinner; boil potatoes for mashed potatoes if you haven't made them ahead; just before meat is ready, begin cooking other vegetables.

And Then

Put a foil tent over the turkey. You now have about an hour to do the remaining cooking:

- If you have a pan of stuffing to bake on the side, put it in now.
- Warm whatever needs to be warmed, including rolls, soups, and casseroles.
- **Mash the potatoes.   Why not make these a day ahead of time? ☐ Make the gravy.**
- Put all the food on the table or buffet. Don't hesitate to press guests into service to put food in bowls, open wine bottles, top up glasses, and dish up cranberry sauce.
- Set out some light appetizers to keep wolves at bay. Serve beverages.
- Enjoy your guests!

Fifteen minutes ahead

☐ Ask someone to fill water glasses while meat is resting and final dishes are being put in serving dishes.

Get a plate and eat! Don't spend the meal running back and forth to the kitchen and end up missing out on the Thanksgiving feast you created.

The before holiday meal grace the family has said for many years:

On this happy day we are thankful for our blessings. We pray for renewed belief in ourselves and each other and hope this bond of love will expand to envelope the entire universe.

10

AND FOR THE JUNIOR COOKS

Chelsea, Connor, a little friend & Max

Song for a Fifth Child

By Ruth Hulburt Hamilton

(A treasured poem, given me by Grandma Millie Snodgrass when Keith was born. Words for a mother to live by.)

Mother, oh mother, come shake out your cloth!
Empty the dustpan, poison the moth,
Hang out the washing and butter the bread, Sew
on a button and make up a bed.
Where is the mother whose house is so shocking?
She's up in the nursery, blissfully rocking!

Oh, I've grown as shiftless as Little Boy
Blue (Lullaby, rockaby, lullaby loo). Dishes
are waiting, and bills are past due (Pat-a-
cake, darling, and peek, peekabo).
The shopping's not done and there's nothing for stew… And
out in the yard there's a hullaballoo.
But I'm playing Kanga and this is my Roo.
Look! Aren't her eyes the most wonderful hue?
(Lullaby, rockaby, lullaby loo.)

Oh, cleaning and scrubbing will wait 'til tomorrow,
But children grow up, as I've learned to my sorrow.
So quiet down, cobwebs. Dust go to sleep.
I'm rocking my baby. Babies don't keep.

Some fun for the younger set:

Edible Play Dough

1 jar peanut butter (18 oz.)
6 Tbsp. Honey
Add non-fat dry milk and knead to right consistency.

Play Doh

2-3 c. flour	2 T. cornstarch
1 c. salt	1 c. warm water
¼ c. oil	vegetable coloring

Cooked Playdough

1 c. flour	½ c. salt
1 cup water	1 tsp. Cream of tartar
1 T. vegetable oil	food coloring

Combine and mix well. Cook over medium heat until mixture forms ball. Cool. Keep wrapped or covered when not in use.

Finger-paints

1 c. Linit Starch with cold water

3   c. boiling water
½ c. soap flakes

Mix starch with enough cold water to make a smooth paste. Add boiling water and cook mixture until it is glossy. Stir in soap flakes. Cool. Will keep a week or longer.

Easel Paint

½ gallon of Vano liquid starch

1   lb. Box white powdered tempera or dry wheat paste or Kalsomine

2   T. powdered alum
4   oz. Tincture green soap

Base: First put in liquid starch. Add white paint and beat well. Add remaining ingredients and beat until smooth and glossy. Not too thick and gooey or too thin and runny. *For Paint*: Add equal parts of base, water and powdered tempera color. [A mostly stay-at-home Mom when children were young, I must have made gallons and gallons of this paint. We had a small schoolroom set up in our basement on Sunnyside in Seattle, complete with school desks and teacher's podium, blackboard, easels, etc. Hours of fun for the preschoolers!…and peace and quiet for the Mom!)

Cloud Pictures

With a bar of mild white soap and a small amount of warm water, make a heavy lather and whip with egg beater until it is the consistency of stiffly-beaten egg whites. Take blobs of soap mixture and fashion simple pictures on dark colored paper: e.g. snowmen, bunny rabbits, seascapes, and cloudscapes take shape naturally. (Pictures get flaky when dry, so they cannot be hung.]

Coal Garden [an early science experiment!]

Place two or three lumps of coal in low dish with a little water. Combine the following and pour over coal slowly:

6 T. common salt
6 T. bluing
6 T. water
1 T. ammonia

For color, drop food coloring over coal with a medicine dropper.

Crystals will soon form. If there are bare spots, drop on a little more ammonia water.

And Now for Some Edibles for Junior Cooks

...and Consumers

Baby Kneads

1 pkg. Dry yeast	1 c. warm water
1/3 c. sugar	1/3 c. oil
3 c. flour	dash of salt

Put the water in a bowl and sprinkle over the yeast. After it settles, mix in the rest of the ingredients and form a ball of dough. Knead the dough for 10 to 15 minutes – this is the part a toddler likes! – on a floured board. Cover the dough and let is rise for one hour (until it has doubled.) This is the part the toddler doesn't like! Knead the dough again. Cut into small balls. Place on greased cookie sheet, cover and let rise. Bake 10 to 12 minutes at 450 degrees. These small rolls will be just right for baby sandwiches!

Ants on a Log

Stuff celery with peanut butter and dot with a row of raisins.

Peanapple

Core an apple. Fill center of apple with a combination of peanut butter and raisins. Great for school lunchbox.

Snow Ice Cream
(A fun project if you happen to be up in the mountains on a snowy day.)

1 cup rich milk
¼ c. Egg Beaters
½ c. sugar 1 tsp. Vanilla dash of
salt
5 cups of clean, fresh snow

Stir all ingredients and eat.

Stuffed Dates

(These bring back fond memories of making these at Christmastime with

Grandma Hoffman, my mother's mother.)

Slit dates open just so that you can remove the pit. Insert sliver of walnut in

place of pit. Close securely and roll in powdered sugar.

Stuffed Walnuts

½ c. peanut butter   ½ c. brown sugar

40 walnut halves   1 c. white sugar

½ c. water (optional)

Mix together peanut butter and brown sugar. With a teaspoon, put a nice-sized lump of peanut butter mix on walnut half. Gently press another half on. Put on cooky sheet. Chill if filling is very soft. You may have to refrigerate the peanut butter mixture until firm, depending on kind of peanut butter you use.

The next part is best done by an adult or older child, as the syrup can be very HOT! Carmelize the white sugar by stirring in a pan over medium heat or add water and heat swirling pan. Cook to honey brown color. Spoon carmelized sugar over walnuts. Let set. (If you work slowly, put sugar pan in a pan of hot water to keep warm.

Popeye's Passion

2 c. drained spinach, chopped
1- 8 oz. Package of cream cheese
½ pt. Sour cream ½ tsp. Nutmeg salt
and pepper to taste

Combine all in a saucepan and
simmer about 15 to 20 minutes, stirring often. Even if you hate spinach, you'll LOVE Popeye's Passion.

Bunny Rabbit Salad

For each serving you will need:

  1 large lettuce leaf
   cold canned pear half
  2 raisins
  1 maraschino cherry
  2 almonds
  1 T. cottage cheese

Put a lettuce leaf on the plate. Put pear half on the leaf. Put raisins on narrow end of pear for the eyes of the bunny. Put a cherry on for his nose. Put almonds on for his ears. Scoop of cottage cheese will look like his furry little tail. Eat and enjoy!

Davis Dump Cake (From our friend, Lisa Wisner)

  1 8-oz. Can crushed pineapple
  1 can cherry pie filling
  1 box lemon cake mix
  1 ½ cubes butter
  ½ c. nuts

Pour pineapple, including syrup, over bottom of a 9 x 13 " pan. Dump cherry filling evenly over this. Dump the dry cake mix and completely cover the pie filling. Slice butter thinly and place on top evenly. Sprinkle nuts over all. Bake at 350 degrees for 45 minutes. Serve warm or cold with whipped cream or ice cream. Yummm!

Luscious Lemonade (From Kurt Wisner, then about age 13)

Prepare a graham cracker crust (1 2/3 c. crushed graham crackers – 11 double graham crackers is about enough, according to Kurt's calculations!) Place in bowl and add ¼ c. sugar, 1 tsp. Grated lemon peel, and 1/3 c. melted butter. Mix with a fork and press into pie plate. Bake at 375 degrees for 8 – 10 minutes. Remove and cool.

Filling: Soften approximately 4 – 5 c. vanilla ice cream and add 8 oz. Of frozen lemonade concentrate. Mix and add several drops of yellow food coloring to get a nice lemony color. Pour into cooled graham cracker crust. Freeze.

Thumbprint Cookies

1 stick butter or 1 c. margarine
1/3 c. sugar
1 c. flour

Blend well and drop about 1 tsp. Per cookie on sheet. Put dimple in center with thumb…not all the way through. Fill with jam, jelly, cinnamon sugar, etc. Bake at 375 degrees for about 10 minutes.

Banana Smoothy

1 cup orange juice   ¼ c. milk
¼ c. Egg Beaters   1 tsp. Sugar
½ to 1 banana, peeled and cut into chunks

Combine all ingredients in blender. Beat until foamy and smooth.

(Can substitute pineapple juice for orange juice, omit sugar. Can omit banana, too.)

Toad in Hole…or Shape Toast

1 slice any large bread
1 egg
Cookie cutter (or glass that is smaller than bread size) 1
helpful kid

Cut center out of slice of bread with a cookie cutter. Heat a large skillet and add Pam or butter. Place bread with cut out hole and the cut out shape in skillet separately. Break one egg into hole (or scramble raw egg if desired before putting into center of bread). Cook over medium heat until white sets. Turn egg toast and shaped toast. Cook another minute or so until yolk of egg is desired doneness. Stars, bears…whatever shapes you happen to have make for an exciting breakfast.)

No-Bake Nut Balls

½ c. chunky nut butter (almond or peanut)
½ tsp. Vanilla or almond extract
½ c. honey
½ tsp. Cinnamon
½ c. nuts (almonds or walnuts)
2 c. crispy, puffed rice cereal Coconut
or chopped nuts

Mix nut butter, honey, nuts, vanilla and cinnamon together in a bowl. Add cereal and stir gently until the cereal is well coated. Place a dish of water near the bowl for wetting your hands before forming the mixture into walnut-sized balls. Roll in coconut or chopped nuts. Store in covered container in the refrigerator. Makes about 2 dozen if not too much is consumed during the rolling process.

Caramel Corn

1 c. butter   ½ tsp.
  Soda

2 c. brown sugar   1 tsp. Vanilla
½ c. light or dark syrup   6 qts. Popcorn
1 tsp. Salt

Melt butter over low heat. Stir in brown sugar, corn syrup and salt. Bring to a boil, stirring constantly. Boil over low heat without stirring for five minutes. Remove from heat. Stir in vanilla and soda. Gradually pour over popped corn. Mix well. Turn into 2-3 large, shallow baking pans. Bake 250 degrees for one hour, stirring every 15 minutes or so. Remove from oven. Cool. Break apart. Enjoy!

Old Fashioned Popcorn Balls

(We used to make these at Halloween and give them out before everyone became so paranoid about "spiked" goodies.)

1/3 c. light corn syrup   1/8 tsp. Baking soda
1 ¼ c. molasses   4 qt. Popped corn, standard, or
1 tsp. Butter   microwave, plain

Combine syrup, molasses and butter in a pan over medium heat. Cook, rarely stirring, to a hardball stage, 265 degrees. Remove from heat and immediately add soda. It will foam. Stir thoroughly. Have popcorn ready in a large pot on very low heat. Pour hot molasses mixture over popcorn and stir. Butter hands and quickly (no problem!) and lightly form balls about the size of a medium orange. Place on waxed paper to cool. Wrap individually in clear wrap. For the holidays, tie with ribbon and put in a colorful bowl. Makes about 20 – again, depending on how much the participants consume while forming the balls.

Chelsea (15) and Max (13) and sushi feast they made for us.

AUTHOR BIO

For more about the author, Joan Callaway. read *Invisible to the Eye: The First Forty Years* and *It's an Ill Wind, Indeed...that Blows No Good.*